COLIN O'BRADY

the 12 HOUR WALK

ERNEST FEDERICO

Epigraph

I just went out for a walk lastly finished up to remain out till dusk, for going out, I found, was truly going in.

—JOHN MUIR

PART I

INTRODUCTION

CHAPTER ONE

1 WHAT'S YOUR EVEREST?

The mass of men lead lives of quiet trouble.

—HENRY DAVID THOREAU

Think about how conceivable it is that I let you in on I'd sorted out some way to help you with continuing with a truly fulfilling life.

Envision a situation in which I could send you on a trip that would leave you feeling like you can accomplish basically anything — that would tell you the best way to shed the confining convictions that are holding you down, and then again open your best life.

Here is the best perspective — envision a situation in which you could complete that journey in a single day.

My heart hustled and I endeavored to unwind.

Minutes earlier, a definite strength had prompted me toward the most noteworthy point inclinations of Mount Everest, but in a second everything had changed, breaking my tranquil demeanor.

I was as of now doing combating for my life.

Blue sky went to ominous dull, and what had been a fragile breeze turned out to be clearly hurricanes mile-per-hour contort, practically ignoring me my feet. The snow whipping around my face stung the revealed portions of my skin like 1,000 tiny needles. I couldn't feel my fingers or my toes as the windchill plunged underneath awful sixty degrees.

Held by fear, I found each step hard-obtained. I stumbled through the "Passing Zone," a locale north of 26,000 feet that owed its well known moniker to the way that, at such a level, the human body steadily dies.

"Stop... did you see any dead bodies on Everest?" a silver haired man mentioned me from the corner from the room.

As I continued to share my records of involvement, a consistently expanding number of requests came flying at me.

"How has everything gone out to the bathroom when it was less thirty degrees in Antarctica?"

"Forty-foot grows, in a 28 foot dinghy? How might you get through that?"

The requests were coming at me, left and right — questions I'd heard beforehand, but this time they were being mentioned by a social occasion from massively productive men — shared reserves bosses, present day magnates, and extremely rich individual monetary benefactors. Not at all like the generally more young or tolerably matured individuals who pepper me with requests after my element addresses and other public appearances, these men had shown up at an age where the roads portraying their life's cycle — streets cleared in gold — would overall be in the rearview reflect.

We were arranged around a parlor region table in an enchanting penthouse townhouse on Manhattan's Upper East Side. I was visiting the region to address a couple hundred Wall Street pioneers about mindset, confronting difficulties, and beating hindrances, and I'd been invited here not long before my talk to visit with a select get-together of them — CEOs by and large — in a more private setting.

Two or three minutes earlier, it had been questionable that I'd attempt to make it into this room.

I was running several minutes late as I immediately wandered into the design's rich lobby and searched for the lift.

Behind me I heard a firm voice, "Where do you accept you're going?"

"I'm scrambled toward the penthouse," I cleared up for the attendant who'd suddenly appeared behind the corridor workspace.

"Um, no you're not."

"I'm ordinary," I said. "For a night gathering."

The individual took a gander at me again. I was wearing jeans, low-top Jordan shoes, and a dull T-shirt — not the dress-for-accomplishment clothing he was familiar with seeing. He pulled a piece of paper from his pocket and focused on it circumspectly — some kind of rundown of participants, I imagined. Then, he shook his head in that satisfied way, thinking he'd avowed his extraordinary impression. "Obviously, kid, if you're with cooking, you need to use the assistance lift."

"Maybe you can call higher up," I proposed.

Reluctantly, the attendant got the phone and mumbled something I couldn't precisely hear. Then he hung up and said, "You have a fair evening, sir." With a surge of his hand, he motioned me toward the lifts at the uttermost completion of the corridor.

I emphatically hadn't guessed that my hosts ought to give a five star gathering, yet neither did I completely consider I'd have to bob groups just to be allowed higher up. I'll surrender, my conviction was a piece shaken as I wandered into the lift. It was one of those crazy luxurious Manhattan structures where the lift opened clearly into the townhouse — for this present circumstance, a palatial home with staggering viewpoints on the city, sitting above Central Park.

At the point when out of the lift, I wandered into a room wherein seven or eight men mixed over drinks. They were perfectly prepared, wearing extraordinarily modified suits, and — I truly needed to see — some wore watches worth more than it had cost to help my last endeavor. One praiseworthy individual pushed toward me rapidly and introduced himself as my host.

"So cheerful you could make it, Colin," he said, enduringly shaking my hand. He had all the earmarks of being genial, yet there was in him something of the caretaker's mindset. I recognized he was examining my choice of apparel.

As I took a seat at an enormous oval table spread out with cleaned silverware, a waiter wandered over to fill my wineglass.

Our host thumped his own jewel glass, and the room fell calm as everyone died down into a seat.

"By and large we as a whole here know each other," the host said — both to me and the rest of the social event. "We've been screwing each other out of plans for an impressive period of time."

The line was followed by a surge of nice laughing, backslaps, and hollers of "Hear, hear!"

Yet again there followed another piece of glass-ringing from the host, and as the room quieted, he said, "Regardless, I figured it would be truly shrewd if we evaded the table and introduced ourselves."

Exclusively, every guest shared a line or two of show. As they spoke, I started to feel that they'd showed up through Central Casting. They were all male, all white, around 65, all continued on from the best schools and spilling with cash.

It wasn't my normal gathering.

Indeed, I'd been raised solid areas for by and free women — my mother, my five additional laid out sisters, and my grandmother. Besides, as of now I was hitched to another strong woman — my soul mate, Jenna Besaw — who kept up with our associations and helped with figuring out every single detail of our exercises.

Zeroing in on no women on this evening, it appeared to be something huge was missing.

As the introductions continued, I pondered what I'd say when I had the floor. As it ended up actually working, I'd gone to Yale, like a lot of the men who'd recently spoken — and I'd even filled in as a Wall Street items trader for an extraordinarily short stretch after graduation. So my course of action at first was to pursue shared conviction. Anyway by then I really check myself out. Shared view? Who was I kidding? Before Yale, I'd been an administration financed school kid from Portland, Oregon, raised by a blended gathering of bloom kid watchmen in a lower common region of the city. When the Yale swim tutor called to select me, my most paramount request was "Yale... where might that at any point be?"

For sure, I was appreciative for my tutoring, but during my four years in New Haven I'd expected to make scarcely to the point of getting by painting houses the whole summer and contingent upon grants and awards to bear the expense of books and instructive expense. On a very basic level, I was thoroughly awkward at Yale (a fitting comparability, taking into account all that time in the pool!), and consequently, I never really felt like I had a spot.

"Great to be here, everyone," I said, when it was my chance to talk. "My name's Colin, and I'm a competitor and a business visionary."

Alright, I thought. That ought to cover it. I settled back and hung tight for the discussion to rapidly continue on toward macroeconomic strategy, securities exchange patterns, or whatever else these Wall Street titans typically visited about.

All things considered, what followed was an abnormal quietness, flagging that I hadn't verged on covering it.

Fortunately, our host stepped in to save me. "Hang on a second, people," he said. "This is Colin O'Brady, the undeniably popular voyager, and there's significantly more going on behind the scenes."

I grinned timidly and lifted my wineglass to the gathering, as though in hello, while the host talked me up.

"Colin has broken ten world records," he said. "He's investigated probably the most limit and remote corners of the planet! Also, lived to tell the story!"

Our host happened more meticulously, let the gathering know how I'd completed the Explorers Grand Slam in world record time, continuously summiting the tallest top on every one of the seven landmasses, and finishing undertakings toward the North and South Poles. Without stopping, he transferred how I'd pulled a 375-pound sled alone across the expanse of land of Antarctica to finish the world's most memorable performance, unsupported, and completely human-fueled crossing of the frozen mainland. Furthermore, he depicted my reality first intersection of the Drake Passage in a dinghy.

"What's more, he's not only a competitor," he proceeded. "He's likewise had a lot of progress with a few undertakings, had his hand in a few enormous scope projects in Hollywood, is a New York Times top of the line creator, and runs a charitable working with schoolkids. He'll educate us regarding this in the feature he's providing for our gathering tomorrow, yet I requested him here this evening so some from us could get to casually know him somewhat more. He's a seriously surprising young fellow, as you will all before long learn. Furthermore, he did all of this after a terrible mishap when specialists let him know he'd at no point ever walk regularly in the future. That was in Thailand, right, Colin?"

Jeez, I thought, a piece humiliated by this extended introduction. This person is great. He'd unquestionably gotten his work done, however I couldn't resist the opportunity to snicker inside at his remark about my age. I was, all things considered, a lot nearer to middle age than to some snot-nosed late school graduate. Be that as it may, to this gathering, I surmise, I was still particularly a "young fellow."

I gestured and said, "That's right, Thailand. I've never been more apprehensive."

At the point when the host was done with his drumroll, his visitors, as opposed to getting back to their monetary discussions as I'd half-anticipated, turned their undivided focus toward me and began peppering me with questions.

"Look," I expressed, attempting to address that inquiry concerning the dead bodies on Mount Everest. "Everest is a perilous spot. I was lucky to in any case come to the culmination in the wake of enduring that unforeseen tempest, however the day I contacted the main three individuals passed on. I wasn't moving with them. I didn't know them actually. Be that as it may, they all kicked the bucket doing what I was doing, around the same time I was making it happen."

I stopped — not to let the second hit home or give it any more weight than it had all alone, however to accumulate my feelings. Indeed, even following four years, I was unable to recount the tale of my most memorable Everest climb without remembering the power of what I'd experienced.

"It's hard," I at last said. "You're laughing in the face of danger. It's reasonable what the stakes are, what can occur. However, it's in those minutes that I feel generally invigorated."

The men around the table knew those minutes. Perhaps not life-and-demise minutes, but rather minutes when everything is on the line. At the point when poo gets genuine.

"So how'd you get into this existence of experience?" was the following inquiry terminated at me.

"It was dependably my fantasy to climb Everest," I said. "Since I was a youngster. I never knew how I would arrive, yet when I arrived at that highest point, my longing to continue to investigate became unquenchable."

In occurrences like this, I savored the chance to reverse the situation and request the gathering one from my number one inquiries.

"I find adolescence dreams are so telling. I've been lucky to satisfy a considerable lot of mine. I envision the greater part of you have also. Tell me, what was your experience growing up dream? What's your Everest?"

I paused for a moment and sat tight for a whirlwind of reactions, yet I got back... nothing.

As I checked the room, the visitors generally appeared to turn away, cautious not to look me in the eyes. Interestingly the entire night they were held, unsocial, maybe even timid. I was stunned.

What's your Everest?

An inquiry ordinarily welcomes an interesting discussion about dreams satisfied, and, indeed, it here and there lights weak comments about dreams hidden. On this evening, in any case... crickets. So I let this line of addressing slide as these very rich people reversed the situation back on me, which was what they appeared to like.

After the night had run its course, and the sweet plates had been cleared, I remained to say my farewells. As I was going to get on the lift to leave, I felt a hand on my arm. I thought back and saw a face I perceived from around the table, having a place with a man who'd been basically quiet all through the supper. The man appeared to be 10 years or so more seasoned than different visitors — perhaps mid-seventies or even eighty. He was white-haired, and thin, yet his eyes had this sort of rheumy look that offered him as somebody who perhaps was counting the days he had left.

"Maybe I can have a snapshot of your time, Colin," he said, attracting me close, away from the others.

"Better believe it, sure," I said, not exactly knowing what's in store.

"I need to apologize for my companions here," he said, demonstrating the others. "You'd posed us a vital inquiry, and nobody appeared to need to reply. About our experience growing up dreams."

"There's compelling reason need to apologize," I said. "Perhaps it was excessively private of an inquiry for this gathering."

He snickered. "For the vast majority of us, yes," he said. "For my purposes, as well, though it pains me to say so. Yet, I so value your time, and your viewpoint, that I should enlighten you a little something concerning myself. It feels significant."

My interest was aroused.

The elderly person proceeded to let me know how when he was a youngster, he used to go to a day camp in upstate New York, where he swam and climbed and rowed around the lake in a skiff. "There isn't a day that goes by when I don't ponder being back on that skiff," he said. He stopped for a beat, and I got the inclination he was proceeding with caution. "That question you asked us," he at last said, " 'What's your Everest?' I can't help thinking about what might have occurred in my life assuming that I'd thought about that as a more youthful man. Assuming I'd really had the get up and go to pursue it. What a valuable gift you've given yourself, to dare to pursue your fantasies and make them work out."

"You're correct about that, sir," I said. "It is valuable. However, shouldn't something be said about you? Posing yourself a similar inquiry is rarely past the point of no return."

"I'm worried about the possibility that that opportunity has arrived and gone for me," he said.

"No lack of regard, sir," I expressed, "yet there's no clock on our deepest desires."

Reluctant to leave this person draping underneath the heaviness of his incomplete considerations, I put the inquiry to him once more. I said, "When you were a kid, when you were a more youthful man, what did you fantasy about becoming one day? What apparently unthinkable objective did you believe was barely too far?"

I was paralyzed by this man's reaction. He shook his head and held out his hands, palms up — the non-verbal communication of weakness. He said, "I sincerely don't recollect. I could remain here and say I needed to play for the Yankees, or become a space explorer, and it would sound great and perhaps draw near to it, however it wouldn't be reality. For a really long time, I got so up to speed in what I assumed I needed to do that I quit paying attention to my heart."

Then, at that point, he inclined in and completed his thinking with a murmur. "I've made a ton of cash in my life, Colin," he said, with barely any hot air. "I'm rich past the vast majority's most extravagant fantasies. Be that as it may, I'd exchange everything for the opportunity to contrastingly return and perhaps get things done over a bit."

I might have cried — and as I looked into, I saw that my new companion was getting a little watery-peered toward himself.

"Guarantee me something," the man said, as he shook my hand in separating. "Continue doing what you're doing. Continue to pursue your joy. Continue to follow that story within you."

At that time, it wasn't obvious to me what this man had lost — perhaps it was the effortlessness he once knew as a youngster, or the tranquility he'd tracked down on that lake, or the chance of what lay ahead. Anything it was, in spite of the outer appearances of having everything, he'd needed something different out of life, something else, and he'd reasoned that I'd some way or another found where he was going wrong.

As I rode the lift down to the entryway, I thought about the Thoreau quote I used to open this section: "The mass of men lead lives of calm distress." It's one of my extremely most loved statements, a convincing update that an excessive number of us will settle — to abandon our fantasies. An excessive number of us are kept down by restricting convictions, unfit to escape our own heads and focus on carrying on with our best lives. Thoreau's line is likewise one of the most misquoted in American writing, in light of the fact that a many individuals offer this form: "Most men lead lives of calm urgency kick the bucket with their tune still inside them." Thoreau never composed that last part, at the same time, at that exact second, that was the expression that rang through my head.

In numerous ways, the book you grasp is my reaction to that new contemplative trade with a lament filled man. It's my approach to satisfying the commitment he requested that I make, to continue pursuing my happiness and following the story inside me. However, my bigger objective is to spread this message so particularly that whatever number individuals as could reasonably be expected exchange day to day routines of calm franticness for lives of profound satisfaction. I've fostered an instrument to assist individuals with doing that... to assist you with doing that.

Is your tune still inside you? Are your fantasies unfulfilled?

Climbing Mount Everest was my experience growing up dream, however you probably had — or have — an alternate dream. Tell me, what's going on here? What does your best life resemble? It doesn't need to be an outrageous trial of actual strength or perseverance or about a particular accomplishment. It tends to be about family, profession, music, travel, bliss, satisfaction... making 1,000,000 bucks or saving 1,000,000 lives... whatever makes some kind of a difference for you, anything that's barely too far. Where would you like to go? What is it that you need to achieve? How would you like to spend your days?

This book is intended to assist you with responding to those inquiries, and really give you an unmistakable arrangement to transform those fantasies into the real world. All things considered, as creator Katherine Paterson broadly said, "A fantasy without an arrangement is only a wish."

Stage 1: I really want you to address this inquiry for yourself.

What's your Everest?

Permit yourself to dream, unbounded — indeed, put away whatever else you have going on, anything restricting convictions have kept you down.

Pause for a minute to truly consider it, then, at that point, fill in the clear beneath:

My Everest is .

Hold that fantasy in your heart and turn the page, since I will tell you the best way to overcome your psyche and open your best life. Summiting the mountain you're intended to ascend is way nearer than you naturally suspect.

CHAPTER TWO

THE 12-HOUR WALK

All in all, genuine talk: Why haven't you arrived at the culmination of your own Mount Everest?

That tune within you — for what reason is it still overlooked?

What's preventing you from carrying on with your best life?

My speculation is you're being kept down by one of the numerous accounts you're presumably telling yourself.

Your interior talk resembles, "I'm not carrying on with my best life on the grounds that... "

"I need more time."

"I need more cash."

"I don't have the right companions."

"I don't have the foggiest idea what to do."

"I'm anxious about falling flat."

"I disdain being awkward."

You acknowledge these accounts as insights, however imagine a scenario where I let you know that they were lies. Lies, pardons, safeguard systems — call them anything you desire. Here in this book, I'm deciding to call them restricting convictions. They're simply that, convictions, and convictions can be changed, adjusted, and overwritten.

You choose. You are the story you tell yourself.

In the pages that follow I'll uncover the keys to overcoming your brain and creating new tales about yourself. These keys will permit you to foster what I call a:

Conceivable MINDSET

an engaged perspective that opens an existence of boundless conceivable outcomes.

With a Possible Mindset you'll have the option to arrive at culminations, yearnings, and objectives that have everlastingly appeared to be far off. You'll be outfitted with the instruments to break liberated from what's been keeping you down.

By embracing a Possible Mindset you'll before long understand that all that you've at any point longed for is, truth be told, conceivable.

A Possible Mindset isn't something that simply a limited handful individuals can have — a remarkable inverse. Everybody has the capacity to prepare their brain utilizing a couple of straightforward advances that I'll show you in this book. When you wrap up perusing the last page, you'll be well on the way to making elevated degrees of progress and, generally significant, tracking down profound satisfaction.

The direction I'll share isn't hypothetical, it's been fashioned by my genuine encounters. It comes from really having been in the field — from fizzling, and falling, and getting scraped up en route. It comes from grappling with similar restricting convictions you're all managing yet figuring out how to conquer them and flourish.

At its zenith this book will leave you with a solitary test, something you can achieve in a solitary day... an encounter that will make the way for carrying on with your best life right away.

I've fostered this one-day solution to cleanse you of restricting convictions and demonstrate to you that you have the ability to move to a Possible Mindset to accomplish anything.

On the whole, before I share that solution, I will let you know how I arrived...

It was May 2020, only a couple of months after that elegant Manhattan supper. The world was in lockdown — in the firm grasp of a pandemic we didn't yet have any idea. My significant other, Jenna, and I were following the stay-at-home order with our canine — a perky wheaten terrier named Jack — at my family's lodge on the Oregon Coast, in the town of Manzanita.

Like the existences of every other person on the planet, our own had been waiting since mid-March. I'd recently distributed my most memorable book, just to find my book visit cut off. My feature talking commitment were dropped. My next endeavor? Likewise dropped.

It was a stressing, disconnecting time. Jenna and I made an honest effort to proceed with our work and to look forward to different undertakings and ventures, never truly knowing when our lives would return to "ordinary." We addressed our loved ones and saw them over Zoom, however we hadn't chatted with any other individual face to face for quite a long time.

In certain regards, life was sweet and rich. We had one another. Had opportunity and energy to reflect... There was an ideal opportunity to relax. But the "on-hold" part of our lives was choking. It was basically impossible to be aware if, when, or how we'd return to previously.

The setting made this difficult situation a ton smoother, that's what i'll say. I'd continuously cherished the Oregon Coast. It was an exceptional spot — considerably more unique now since it offered such a tremendous scene in the midst of a period of lockdown. The sea shores were level, wide, hopeless — in no way like Southern California, say, where they're packed with individuals, overflowing with daylight and activity. Our sea shores are vacant and long, frequently extending for seven miles or more, past precipices and tough stone arrangements — and during those dim, discouraging weeks from the beginning in the pandemic there was many times no other person around.

It was late in the day. Woefully, I hadn't changed out of my nightgown. Another erratic COVID day had recently gulped me. I was unable to shake the funk that had grasped me since the world was placed on hold. I pulled a book off the rack and plunked down on the chair close to the window, yet I was unsettled and couldn't zero in on the words before me. Occupied, I gazed upward from my book and gazed out at the sea. A situation was unfolding. The breeze was kicking up. I could see the sand, cyclone like, whipping along the shore.

The twirling sand helped me to remember the snow that had spiraled across the Antarctic ice eighteen months sooner, and I was in a flash moved. In those days, I was attempting to pull a 375-pound sled across a bone chilling, forsaken field of 932 miles, from one finish of the mainland to the next — an unsupported, completely human-fueled, solo intersection of the whole expanse of land of Antarctica, something that had never been achieved.

I wasn't simply hustling history, as it ended up. I was secured in a straight on fight with Captain Louis Rudd, a British Special Forces warrior and veteran polar pioneer, who was making his own performance endeavor to accomplish this noteworthy world first.

I recalled that it had required a few days for me to conform to the crazy cold of the frozen landmass... that my goggles had been frozen by snot and tears... that I was unable to see a thing, or hear myself think underneath the wailing breezes. For the most part, I recollected that powerless yet thrilling sensation of being totally alone for a long time, in no place.

My brain streaked back to a particular second on the ice — one that made a huge difference.

"Perhaps you can go for an additional hour tomorrow," Jenna recommended through the static of my SAT telephone. "You know, make up some mileage. Somewhat consistently."

"I previously told you," I said. "I can't pull my sled for over ten hours out of each day."

In my voice, I knew, Jenna could hear how crushed I was after only five days on the ice. "It's excessively weighty," I said despondently. "I'm destroyed."

Jenna was attempting to direct a portion of consolation, and to help me issue tackle my direction back into the race, after I'd so immediately fallen behind Captain Rudd on Day One — however I was never going to budge on firm furnishing her energy with my restricting convictions.

"I can't go any more!" I yelled furiously into the frozen tremendousness — and into the SAT telephone. My resentment wasn't aimed at Jenna, obviously. She was the most steady accomplice I might have requested. She'd been instrumental in the preparation of everything about this undertaking — and presently, in the revising of those intends to oblige this surprising test from this unforeseen challenger, my disappointment with my own shortcoming had arrived at a sort of edge of boiling over. I stressed that my mission to turn into the main human to make this crossing was at that point ill-fated.

My karma changed the extremely following day when I some way or another got up to speed to Captain Rudd interestingly. I saw his red tent somewhere far off through a whiteout and acknowledged I'd acquired ground on him than I'd recently suspected.

There followed a short, serious trade with Captain Rudd on the ice soon thereafter. We both knew the stakes of this: several years sooner an endeavor at a comparable performance crossing had finished in lethal misfortune.

"Commander Rudd, I don't wish you any hostility over here, yet we're both attempting to turn into the first to finish this intersection, and the expectation is to be distant from everyone else. So let this be the last time we speak," I expressed, attempting to extend a quality of certainty notwithstanding my negative inward exchange.

For the following long while, we were secured in a quiet, unacknowledged fight, as every one of us attempted to say something of solidarity and predominance. Two men, hauling weighty sleds, side by side across the interminable white, matching each other step for step as the hours delayed, as voiceless prizefighters exchanging blows.

Some place in these strained minutes, I arrived at the ten-hour mark on my day's work, my standard place to pause. I was totally depleted, yet I was reluctant to allow it to show. I looked over at Captain Rudd and it seemed he had zero desire to stop either, so I went ahead. I dug further than at any other time, tapping stores of solidarity and will I didn't realize I had, decided not to tap out that day until Captain Rudd stuffed it in.

Eventually, all that ultimately mattered was which one of us flickered first.

Following eleven hours, Captain Rudd waved the white banner. I saw him stop to set up his tent, and I inhaled a long moan. In any case, I wouldn't allow myself to stop. Skipper Rudd's halting didn't allow me to stop myself — rather, it lit something in me to continue onward. Out of nowhere, still up in the air to push one more hour, to lay out my most memorable genuine lead in this almost thousand-mile race, and in that defining moment second I understood that Captain Rudd's presence on the ice had constrained me to reexamine my restricting convictions and alter my attitude.

I went from figuring I can't to demonstrating I can... all on the rear of this far-fetched fight.

The following day, to keep up with my lead and maybe expand on it, I logged an additional twelve hours pulling my weighty burden. The day from that point forward, same thing. I told myself on the off chance that I could do it once, I could definitely do it two times, and afterward again from that point forward, etc... twelve-hour days, each and every day for the following 48 days.

Back in the lodge, in Oregon, that memory lifted me from my irredeemable state of mind. I got to believing that albeit the consistent twelve-hour days trudging alone across the ice had at first addressed the external furthest reaches of my solidarity and confidence in myself, in the end I'd tracked down more rapture, quiet, and reason in those twelve hours every day than I'd at any point known. Walking across the ice, my psyche had never been so clear and my life had never felt so boundless and satisfying. Was there a method for finding that mentality again without going back to Antarctica?

I crept into bed close to Jenna that evening, feeling somewhat lighter, somewhat less disheartened — as though an internal light were glinting with a groundbreaking thought, another concentration.

The following morning, I awakened more empowered than I'd been in weeks. I leaped up and enthusiastically reported, "I'm taking a walk. Day in and day out! Twelve hours."

Obviously, taking a walk was generally typical. It was one of a handful of the exercises permitted during COVID lockdown. Thus, Jenna and I had logged endless miles all over that ocean side along with Jack, however toward the beginning of today I had the drive to head out performance.

Jenna could perceive I was onto something; she'd seen me like this previously. She streaked me a reassuring grin.

"I will evaluate another idea I have permeating," I said. Also, very much like that I limited out the front entryway in view of no particular objective.

It was a dark day, cold for May, with a lively breeze moving along the shore break. I was courageous by the grim climate, notwithstanding, and before long forgot about time as the hours ticked by. My contemplations ran free.

Sooner or later, I felt my telephone buzz in my pocket. Naturally I went after it, and afterward I pulled my hand back. Hadn't I had sufficient screen time as of late? Destruction looking over the news, monitoring virtual entertainment, marathon watching Netflix — day to day existence had turned into an apparently steady stream of Face Time assembles and Zoom conferences.

I needn't bother with my telephone for this walk, I thought, and exchanged it into flight mode.

Notwithstanding my underlying energy, I didn't figure this sounds simple. At the point when I was out there on the ice in Antarctica, I had no real option except to accompany myself peacefully. Here on this dark May morning, I was deliberately looking for isolation to mull over life, again without any interruptions.

As I strolled, a consistent stream of contemplations rose. I positively was appreciative for everything that appeared to be going right: my relationship, my local area, my well being. In any case, similarly, I was attempting to speak the truth about what left me feeling unfulfilled. But then it was anything but a sad inclination. As I filtered my brain's hazier corners, something about the setting of the 12-Hour Walk — being turned off, untethered from the day to day disorder — gave me the space and solidarity to imaginatively analyze my restricting convictions and reorient my attitude toward carrying on with my best life.

As the sun started dropping into the sea, I hurried up to attempt to make it home before dim.

Jenna met me at the entryway with an embrace. "How was it?" she said eagerly.

"It was an enlightening encounter. There's something to this idea. Truly, I feel far improved than I have in months. That walk was exactly what I really wanted. I figure anybody could profit from a 12-Hour Walk," I said, embracing her.

I grinned as Jack bounced up to welcome me, glad for me to be home too.

So that is the way I thought of this thought for the 12-Hour Walk, however to be clear direct: this book isn't about me, it's about you.

You are the legend of this story. I'm just here to direct you as you require on a one-day venture that will open a Possible Mindset and change your life until the end of time.

The Walk could sound basic — and in a great deal of ways it is — yet there's power in effortlessness. What's more, it could be said, sorcery. Undoubtedly, the bearings are easy to follow:

1. COMMIT — Pick a day on your schedule to finish the 12-Hour Walk by visiting: 12hourwalk.com/commit.

2. RECORD — Before you set out on your walk, record a brief video of yourself to express your expectations. What restricting convictions would you like to quietness? Portray how you desire to feel when you complete the 12-Hour Walk.

3. Turn off — Turn your telephone on quite mode prior to beginning your 12-Hour Walk. The 12-Hour Walk is intended to be taken alone, with no outer sources of info — no mates, no earphones, no digital broadcasts, no music, no email, no messages, no online entertainment — for the whole twelve hours. Save your telephone with you for wellbeing, however use it just to record a fast video or compose a note to consider later.

4. WALK — Begin your 12-Hour Walk. Very much like life, you pick the objective. Stay outside for twelve hours, strolling peacefully. The setting you're strolling in needn't bother with to be totally quiet, however you do. It is the way to Maintain your quiet. Encompassing city clamor is OK.

5. REST — The 12-Hour Walk isn't a race. Enjoy as the need might arise. It doesn't make any difference in the event that you walk one mile or fifty; as long as you continue moving when you can, you're winning.

6. REFLECT — Record a video as you finish your 12-Hour Walk. Ask yourself: How would you feel? What did you find? What restricting convictions did you survive? What do you presently feel equipped for with your Possible Mindset?

Basic right? All things considered, perhaps not all that quick. I see you not too far off through the opposite side of the pages previously attempting to work yourself out of this, asking why in the world you got this book in any case. I see your restricting convictions folding their arms over your psyche as you read this.

You're sharing with yourself:

"I'm not adequately fit to stroll for twelve hours."

"I have children, and a bustling position, I lack the opportunity to require an entire day to myself... and regardless of whether I, I certain as damnation wouldn't spend it strolling alone peacefully."

"Quietness? Being separated from everyone else? I'd get sooooo exhausted... and that long, alone with simply my contemplations — that sounds awkward. No, that is not so much for me."

In all honesty, you'll track down that the questions, fears, and pushbacks you're appointing to the 12-Hour Walk are really exactly the same restricting convictions that continue to keep you down all through all parts of your life. The restricting convictions that hold you back from turning into the best, most satisfied form of you.

That is where the remainder of this book comes in. Every part will separate one of the ten most normal restricting convictions we face, and demonstrate the way that you can vanquish your psyche to defeat it. We will make a trip together to energizing spots at the edges of the world, yet in addition to unnerving spots to us. Furthermore, you will scarcely believe, I won't gloss over anything.

You'll be more grounded for it.

Threatened? Try not to be. You're in good company. I'll be directing you on this excursion constantly, so toward the finish of these pages, you'll be prepared to require on the 12-Hour Walk and embrace a Possible Mindset, relinquishing your restricting convictions, as you step into your best life.

Most self improvement and self-improvement books miss the mark since they live and bite the dust on the page. All the time, they're loaded up with helpful statements and hypothetical beliefs to consider, yet there will never be actually a chance for the peruser to follow up on anything.

Just paying attention to me and trusting me won't bring about your taking on a Possible Mindset. Illustrations like that seldom stick. What will compel this book's illustrations stick will be your own experience finishing the 12-Hour Walk. You'll feel these illustrations, live them, inhale them, and incorporate them. They'll be carved so profoundly into you that there'll be no real way to at any point neglect.

I'm requesting you to make a tiny speculation from your time. At some point. That is all — a solitary day. Comprehend, I'm not requesting that you give that day to me. It has a place with you.

Contribute one day, vanquish your brain, and open your best life.

The 12-Hour Walk is for anybody. It doesn't make any difference your age, wellness level, or situation. After my stroll along the Oregon Coast, I needed to ensure the idea wasn't simply an excessively aggressive thought, however something that anybody could try — so you could say that I drafted some guineas pigs.

The outcomes were consistently certain. From my old school companion who was battling to track down importance in his regular work, to my kid mother by marriage, who was addressing how best to streamline her brilliant years, each individual I've known to finish the 12-Hour Walk has shown up toward the end goal in a greatly improved place than when they began.

Assuming that you're as of now carrying on with your best life, there's compelling reason need to peruse further. Help me out and put this book down and continue doing your thing.

Until the end of us who actually need a lift to get unstuck, read on. Your best life is standing by.

PART II
LIMITING BELIEFS

CHAPTER THREE

Restricting BELIEF: "I HATE BEING UNCOMFORTABLE."

I grasped the paddles with all that I had.

The waves were coming in fierce sets — blast! blast! blast! — hurling our little boat with a fierce power that lifted us from the surface and cannonballed us back down.

In the wake of getting rammed on all sides by forty-foot enlarges for as long as hour, I was totally doused. As the freezing water insulted me, sending shudders through my body, the salt water consumed both my noses and the rear of my throat, leaving me heaving for air.

As each wave hit, I thought about what it might feel want to suffocate in these frigid waters — and as the wave pummeling proceeded, I contemplated whether I was suffocating as of now.

We were in a little 28 foot, open-frame dinghy named Ohana, just four feet wide and riding only two feet over the water, endeavoring to cross the world's generally hazardous stretch of sea — in a savage, relentless tempest.

My whole spotlight was on my paddles, and it seemed to me like the sea's whole spotlight was on isolating me from them. At this point my hands had been frozen into a sort of tight clamp grasp, got into a clawlike position, yet with each strong sprinkle of freezing seawater, the sea appeared to need to smack the paddles from my hands and send us spiraling.

What tormented me at this time — the idea I was unable to shake — was that I'd decided to be here. We'd decided to be here — every one of the six of us. We'd risk our lives to make a trip toward the southernmost tip of South America to endeavor to cross the Drake Passage and arrive at the central area of Antarctica in a sea dinghy. We just had our muscles and coarseness to drive us forward — no engine, no sail. Nobody had at any point finished this approximately 700 mile sea crossing in a completely human-controlled vessel.

This tempest explained to me why.

We'd been paddling in three-man shifts — an hour and a half on, an hour and a half off. Since the flows were areas of strength for so, must be moving 24 hours every day or chance being passed many miles over course. That implied twelve hours of paddling every day, consistently, with twelve hours of discontinuous rest cut into hour and a half lumps — despite the fact that take a stab at "resting" in a small scale hold where you have probably as much space to move as a carcass in a shut casket.

At any rate, that had been the arrangement, in relative quiet. Here, in relative wrath, our goal was to keep the boat went to confront the waves: assuming that we got crashed into by one of these beasts, we were in a bad way.

The skies had gone dark underneath the tempest mists, so we could scarcely see past our paddles. The waves were acquiring in power — as you'd anticipate in a seething storm.

I was on the paddles with Cameron Bellamy, a world record-holding waterman from South Africa, and Jamie Douglas-Hamilton, a Scotsman who himself claimed a few world records in sea paddling. We had us covered to our objective, which implied we were trusting where we were proceeding to confront where we'd been — a helpful representation that underscored the uninformed religiosity we'd put in one another, and this excursion.

Cam woofed out guidelines as the wave overwhelmed us: "Right side! Right side!"

I inclined toward my next stroke, consequences be damned. My arms felt like they had a place with another person.

"Left side! Left side!"

I attempted to match Cam and Jamie as we swung our bodies forward and got through the water — the three of us realizing that a solitary rebel wave could end our excursion.

All of a sudden, our chief, Fiann Paul — an incredibly famous sea rower from Iceland who'd initially considered the thought for this venture — popped his head from the harsh lodge and yelled, "Everyone ready and available! We've must get out the ocean anchor! We can't push into this tempest any longer!"

I was situated in the third position, straightforwardly before the bow lodge, where John Petersen and Andrew Towne, who'd paddled group at Yale, were timing their hour and a half rest span.

I beat on the minuscule way to their lodge from my situated position and shouted, "Ocean anchor! We're putting out the ocean anchor!"

Andrew yelled back, through the lid: "Let us know when we're between waves!"

"We would rather not flood the lodge!" John hollered.

With the frosty salt water ceaselessly sprinkling my uncovered face I was unable to see a lot, so I'd been timing the waves on feel. I thought we had around twenty seconds among expands, and as the following wave roared down on us I shouted to them: "Presently! Presently! Next one's coming! Move, move, move!"

Andrew and John sprang from the lodge onto the little deck, and promptly locked the entryway behind them and got the security ties on their life coats to the rope that ran along the structure — a half beat before the following wave walloped the boat and almost thumped them on their butts.

Andrew was accountable for the ocean anchor, so he pulled it from its dry sack and worked madly, yet carefully, to ensure the ropes weren't tied or tangled.

"Aaagghhh, these gloves!" he shouted following a disappointing couple of moments, as he stripped the flimsy neoprene from his hands with his teeth, trusting his frozen fingers were capable.

As he battled, we continued to get pounded by many waves, shook from one side to another, all over, as the three of us on the paddles attempted to keep our boat adjusted against the grows.

With a help from John and Fiann, Andrew was at last ready to send the ocean anchor — an enormous parachute that spread out underneath the outer layer of the water and held us back from being brushed stunningly off base. At the point when it drew in — unexpectedly, emphatically — it yanked the boat with such power that we were pulled in reverse, similar to a pit bull stifled toward the finish of its chain.

In the wake of finding our equilibrium, we got our paddles and taken hold of the midsection high ropes on the fiberglass boat that prompted the two little lodges at one or the flip side. There we'd brave what was left of the tempest.

As the primary mate, I'd been substituting with Captain Fiann, exchanging shifts the harsh lodge, dealing with the rudder and route. The remainder of the team exchanged, two all at once, in the marginally bigger hold at the bow, yet now that we were adrift anchor we had to bend over. That implied two men in a single hold, and four packed in another. At the point when I'd been separated from everyone else in the harsh lodge beforehand, the space was little to such an extent that even hunkered in a fetal position, my head was simply crawls from the roof. Presently attempting to get away from the tempest, Fiann and I hastily wedged ourselves into the harsh lodge together.

So I was right there, offering these couple of square feet to a six-foot-one, 190-pound Nordic monster who hadn't washed in seven days. Envision stuffing two big boys into the storage compartment of a Honda Civic — you understand everything.

We expected our positions — our arms and legs folded over one another in an abnormal spoon.

We were bone-chilly, bone-drained, soaked, half-sitting in a couple crawls of smelling seawater. Assuming one of us moved, or even jerked, the other one needed to change in accordance with oblige. Because of nausea, I'd vomited a lot of times from the get-go in the journey, so we were washed in the smell of flat regurgitation and ocean ooze and man sweat. More awful, Fiann was prone to eat dried fish that he kept in oil-doused packs, and it was the most incredibly rank-smelling thing of all time!

"This is the way I'm solid," he'd express, squeezing off each nibble while I did whatever it takes not to spew.

We were getting smacked around by a constant attack of waves, our heads pounding against the walls or the floor or one another.

"How much longer, do you think?" I said during one brief break.

"Who is to be aware?" Fiann replied in his cut English.

Inevitably, it began to feel like these long, hopeless minutes could continue forever, yet there was no tapping out. Like I said, we'd all decided to be here. But of the multitude of outrageous circumstances I'd found myself mixed up with throughout the span of my undertakings — from Everest to the icescape of Antarctica — this was one of the most terrible… one of the most challenging to persevere.

I was harming. Terrible. Everywhere. The tight, claustrophobic circumstances inside the hold pushed me to a spot past uneasiness. It was practically horrendous. Strike that: it was horrendous, but I had no real option except to bear it. In addition, I was squeezing and hurting in manners I was unable to address, with no space to move. Everything hurt, from the shooting torments in my fingers to the tingling sensation consuming sensation in my dead toes. It occurred to me that maybe this journey had been ill-fated all along.

There had been warnings all around.

Emotions had been raging among our team in the approach our journey. There were mechanical issues with our boat. The rudder wasn't working as expected during the test column.

The greatest, most clear sign that perhaps we weren't intended to push the Drake Passage was that we were setting out in the center of a Chilean public misfortune. While advancing toward our beginning point, a Chilean Air Force plane crashed in the Drake en route to an army installation close to Antarctica, killing every one of the 38 individuals ready — a horrible bitterness that draped a dark cloud on our takeoff.

As we were on the way from our arranging grounds in Punta Arenas, Chile, to send off our dinghy at Cape Horn, we were surprised by the booming hints of crisis alarms.

"Stand down!" came an incorporeal voice, through a bullhorn. "Stand down!"

I thought back and saw a huge Chilean Navy transport, which appeared to have arisen in the water out of the blue. It had pulled up close by the

Braveheart — the bigger vessel that was conveying our skiff to the beginning line.

The bullhorn, once more: "We are getting on your boat. Clear a path."

Out of nowhere, about six Chilean military officials boarded the Braveheart, conveying enormous weapons. It was alarming, irritating, dreamlike… for the most part strange.

"The Drake Passage is currently a tactical accident site," the head of this gathering reported. "You will follow us to our maritime port and stay there until additional notification."

"Further notification" to Chilean military authorities signified "until after we complete our salvage and recuperation endeavors," which could require weeks, and by then our window to endeavor the intersection would be shut.

I looked on from the scaffold of the Braveheart and attempted to get a handle on the deadlock. On one side we had these strongly serious Chilean Navy authorities, wearing their stark dull outfits with dark berets. On the opposite side we had the Braveheart's group of pungent Kiwi ocean canines considering what was happening and why it had at least something to do with them. Braveheart's commander went this way and that with the tactical authorities, and for some time it appeared as though our task was over before it even began. Fortunately, it was arranged that assuming we consented to change our arranged paddling course marginally we'd be permitted to start our intersection.

Now that I was full into these nearby, sharp quarters at the harsh of the dinghy, getting thrown all over by a furious ocean, I thought back on those dim, tense minutes as a sign of the dull, tense minutes to come.

All in all, what in blazes had we been thinking, paddling our boat through a mass burial ground? How did we not consider this plane accident to be the mother of every single warning?

But we were right here — and here we'd be in the Drake Passage engaging this tempest, for the following long, horrible while.

I went through a fast self-evaluation.

I asked myself, Am I awkward? (Indeed!)

Am I in torment? (Indeed!)

Does what is going on totally suck? (Indeed!)

My brain dashed — from the signs we ought to have seen, to the signs that were currently before me.

One more chilling sign: I peered out the little opening in our lodge entryway and saw through the hazed glass the hazy picture of one of our crewmates. I was unable to see who it was from the get go, so I cleared the buildup off of the little window and inclined in for a more critical look. It was Cam, his arms lashed to one or the other side of the boat, his head being whipped from one side to another each time a wave battered the deck. From the manner in which he sat, from the manner in which he was being jolted powerfully from one side to another, it seemed as though he was being drawn and quartered in a town square.

He might have been cleared over the edge all of a sudden.

However hopeless as it might have been here in the harsh hold with Fiann, conditions were obviously far more terrible until the end of the group.

I got on the radio that permitted us to speak with one another, lodge to lodge. I could barely comprehend that circumstances in their two-man hold in the bow were far more regrettable than what we were persevering in our one-man hold at the harsh.

"What's he doing out there?" I asked. "Cam."

"No space for each of the four of us inside," I heard back. "We're taking movements. Four and a half hours in the lodge, an hour and a half one man on the deck. We'll trade out soon."

"Goodness, man," I said. "That is fucking ruthless."

Then, another voice: "Better one of us out there than four of us in here."

I ended up sympathizing with my partners right across the way. They were in a horrible spot. We as a whole were.

On the whole, we were on ocean anchor for almost 24 hours — an apparently unending stretch in the most hopeless circumstances. Close to the end, I was so ridiculous, so numb, so whipped by these booming waves that I floated off two or three beats — or perhaps I was thumped quickly oblivious by the disturbance. At the point when I woke with a beginning, the tempest had at long last passed. The boat was still — not altogether still, yet at the same time enough. The tearing breezes that had consumed the space like a basic shout were for the most part quiet. Fiann probably sleepy, as well, since he was arriving at a similar place of understanding, at about a similar time, and as we unwound our appendages and opened the harsh hold, we were struck by a surge of splendid daylight. We ventured carefully onto the deck and wondered about the tranquility of the water, the blue of the sky.

Somewhere far off, I recognized a gooney bird taking off above us, and I followed it as it put itself down on the outer layer of the water, right close to our boat — one more advantageous allegory for the weight we'd recently conveyed and had figured out how to save.

Across the way, our crewmates stirred to a similar scene — three of them crawling from the bow lodge and energizing the fourth, who'd been braving the remainder of the tempest on the deck.

Cam, for one's purposes, was strangely in the mind-set to celebrate.

He extended to his full level, and from the manner in which he stood it appeared as though he'd never stood so tall. Like most of us, he was feeling on the edge of rout after the tempest — yet, dissimilar to most of us, he was on a mission to effectively change that.

He held his arms wide, as though embracing the new day, and shouted out, "Young men, I'm taking a dip!" Then he peeled off his wet garments — no simple thing, with the manner in which everything had been doused through and was currently gripping to his skin.

Picture it: this stripped man, revealed in the Drake Passage, in frigid temperatures. It was the most surprising, most humorous, most peculiarly inspiring thing. Most of us looked on and partook in his satisfaction, however we weren't going to go along with him in the water. It was amazingly cold!

Cam dove into the sea with such power the boat shook with his weight, and as we influenced to redress, we were in the sea with him — in soul, in any event. As he swam around fifty feet from the boat in the frigid water that hurried to a profundity more prominent than 10,000 feet, I was struck by the incongruity, all things considered, the very waters that had quite recently impacted us and appeared to need to kill us were currently starting sensations of opportunity and satisfaction.

Honestly, we were quite far from done. At this sweet place of respite, we were at about the midway imprint in our journey. There'd be different tempests, other apparently perpetual stretches stayed in those dreadful lodges. At the point when the weather conditions permitted, we continued our paddling revolutions: an hour and a half on, an hour and a half off. At the point when the weather conditions kicked up once more, we hurried once again into those holds and got back to our common hopelessness.

At last, following twelve days, with the world's most slippery sea miles behind us, we'd almost arrived at the finish of our excursion. The last miles were mystical indeed. Yet again the skies were indeed clear, the water quiet.

On one side of the boat, a humpback whale moved across the surface as though to welcome us.

On the opposite side, many penguins plunge bombarded from their roost on a close by chunk of ice.

My cheeks consumed from the enormous grin put to my face as I took everything in.

Without a doubt, it was quite possibly of the most great, most exciting sight I'd at any point seen. Such overflow! Such stunning normal magnificence!

We'd done it! We'd turn into the principal individuals to at any point finish this intersection in a completely human-fueled skiff. We struggled each of the tempests in the sea and to us, and presently we were here in this Shangri-la, radiating proudly and kinship.

At the point when we could see the coastline of Antarctica —
incidentally on Christmas Day — Andrew gave me a present from one
of our lodge's holds. A flare.

"Land fucking ho!" he said as he lit the flare.

He lit one for every one of us, and we held them up high in win. It was
perfect, marvelous... as far as I might be concerned would be. As far as
I might be concerned must be. Since I'd known from the start, where it
counts, that snapshots of triumph can be fabricated exclusively on top
of snapshots of battle.

HOW THIS STORY APPLIES TO YOU

How would you gauge your days?

I measure my days on a size of 1 to 10, with a 1 being the absolute
worst day and a 10 being awesome, most euphoric, most staggering
day.

This is the way I check it: the recurring pattern of our days resembles
the swing of a pendulum, with the pinnacle bends addressing our 1s and
10s out.

You can't have one without the other. That beast 24 hour storm, being
thrown by the rough waves like a spec of sand in a dust storm, was at
the lower part of the base, the most exceedingly terrible of the most
awful — especially a 1. That day when we at last made land following
an almost fourteen day bad dream adrift, in the hug of that large
number of penguins and whales, that exceptional regular magnificence,
was all the most elite — an outright 10.

But that second as we moved toward the shores of Antarctica could not
have possibly hit me with such groundbreaking power on the off
chance that I hadn't encountered that multitude of earlier hopeless
minutes. You might have moved me to exactly the same spot through
an extravagance voyage transport and shown me similar sights, yet it
could never have felt something similar. Gracious, it could have
enlisted as a 6 or 7, since it was damn perfect, yet what made it an all
out 10 was the battle and distress I persevered en route — which was
all important to accomplish an objective of this size.

What I've understood is that our 1s and our 10s are associated. To completely encounter our most elevated high, we need to contact our least low... and we must propel ourselves from what I call the "zone of agreeable carelessness," somewhere in the range of 4 and 6. The miserable truth is, that is where a large portion of us reside more often than not.

A more profound truth is that by fostering a Possible Mindset we can prepare our brains to partake in the 1s — or, in any event, to anticipate them. Truly. I don't avoid those snapshots of agony and misery, since I realize they'll take me to snapshots of unadulterated delight. A mantra that has helped me — and that I believe you should keep in mind — is my variant of the statement at this section's start: Pain is required, enduring is discretionary.

Recollect through your own insight and review your snapshots of outright euphoria and fulfillment and you'll see that your 10s were based on the rear of stresses and strains — your 1s. Embrace the 1s. A satisfied life — your satisfied life — relies upon that.

In numerous ways, our cutting edge society drives us to the zone of agreeable lack of concern. A great many people are trapped in the 4–6 territory and pass up the full experience life brings to the table. We're hesitant to face risk challenges get through troubles that could undermine our balance and disturb the consistency of our days. The American Dream, for instance, is tied in with purchasing an agreeable house in suburbia, working all day, and being content with about fourteen days of excursion.

However, is that actually your fantasy? I accept the greater part of us strive after more — some kind of experience that will gauge what we're truly prepared to do.

A lot of life is agreeing to great not extraordinary, with a ton of time spent in the "eh, can't say anything negative" zone. Suppose you have a regular work. You don't cherish it, you don't can't stand it. It's something you do to cover the bills. At some point, your manager could shout at you for missing a cutoff time or wrecking a show, however that day is simply a 4 on your pendulum swing, since you couldn't care less about your occupation for your supervisor's failure to enroll as a 1.

Suppose you begin to excel at work. You're up for an advancement, or some sort of industry grant, however the acknowledgment doesn't actually push you past a 6 — once more, since you're not so profoundly contributed that these distinctions have a significant effect.

One final representation: you're hanging with your dearest friends, drinking lagers, giving a shout out to your #1 football crew on an end of the week evening. The day could rate a 6 on the off chance that your group ends up winning. In the event that your group loses, it's a 5 — on the grounds that, hello, you were with your brothers. Or on the other hand perhaps it's a 4, in the event that you lost cash on the game.

We really want to propel ourselves, challenge ourselves. We want to go from great to incredible, to trudge through a troublesome times to arrive at unadulterated delight and elation.

Distress is much of the time the cost that should be paid to accomplish satisfaction.

I don't encounter my 10s regardless of my 1s. I experience them in light of my 1s… and you will as well.

Pause for a minute to contemplate your relationship to the 1s. Do you go out as you would prefer to stay away from them? Assuming you do, you're in good company — a great many people would prefer to evade the distress that comes from facing challenges or taking to courses of action. As far as some might be concerned, the gamble reward condition doesn't necessarily add up — meaning, it's not worth getting through supported difficulty just to taste a snapshot of triumph.

In any case, here's a news streak: the prize that is sitting tight for you on the opposite side of this hard stretch merits the cost of arriving.

Individuals inquire as to whether I'm anxious about death. They catch wind of my undertakings in a skiff in the Drake, or on the ice in Antarctica, or on the bone chilling pinnacles of K2 or Everest, and need to understand what's going through my brain when I'm facing it, in the teeth of peril.

My response quite often amazes them.

"Clearly, I would rather not bite the dust," I say. "Yet, what I'm truly terrified of isn't living."

We invest our energy unfortunate of encountering the 1s, yet consider the possibility that rather we decided to fear living in the zone of agreeable smugness consistently. Consider the possibility that what we truly ought to fear is the gauge state of "fine and dandy" and "OK" or "adequate".

Please accept my apologies, yet entirely "sufficient" is simply not adequate. Not so much for me. Not really for you.

Feeling invigorated in snapshots of agony is definitely more fascinating than simply existing in the deadness of the center. It's fine to visit your usual range of familiarity now and again. It's essential — to revive, re-energize, pull together, as a matter of fact. However, let's not mince words: Growth occurs outside the safe place; it occurs in that madly confined harsh lodge in a tenacious tempest. It happens when you risk all that to go into business. It happens when you step back and watch your little girl go across the road without help from anyone else for the absolute first time.

It happens when you embrace a Possible Mindset by abandoning the zone of agreeable lack of concern and entering more hazardous waters, letting yourself know that the distress you're taking on can be explored and that the 10 you look for lies up ahead.

KEY TAKEAWAY

Embrace the 1s

Is it safe to say that you are carrying on with an existence of calm distress? Is it safe to say that you are caught in the zone of agreeable lack of concern, stuck somewhere in the range of 4 and 6, agilely attempting to try not to feel any uneasiness? Unshackle yourself from that attitude. Look for difficulties that take you beyond your usual range of familiarity. In this manner you'll encounter some distress — maybe even a couple 1s — however trust me, it'll be in every way worth the effort when you luxuriate in your next 10.

HOW THIS APPLIES TO YOUR 12-HOUR WALK

Decision time: this walk will not be simple. You may be agreeable for the initial five or six hours. However, there'll be the point at which your feet will begin to hurt. Your legs could squeeze. Persevere through it.

Embrace the aggravation. Keep in mind, torment is obligatory, enduring is discretionary. Praise the 1s you'll hit in Hour 7, Hour 8, Hour 9... and continue onward. Battle through the low minutes and allowed them to convey you to the completion. The 10 you'll encounter when you return to your front entryway will motivate you to keep deliberately getting out of your usual range of familiarity to carry on with your most satisfied life.

WITH A POSSIBLE MINDSET,

I love getting out of my usual range of familiarity since it prompts satisfaction.

CHAPTER FOUR

Restricting BELIEF: "I'M NOT A _____."

Human experience amounts to much more than tracking down yourself. Life is tied in with making yourself.

—GEORGE BERNARD SHAW

"Goddammit!" I shouted out, holding onto something as my boat began to flip.

I hung on all that could be expected, battling the unavoidable, and when it seemed as though I was going to upset I took a full breath and held it as I went down with the boat.

The boat fell on top of me — a wreck of paddles and fiberglass above. I mixed to liberate myself from the foot lashes at the vessel's front, so I wouldn't be caught under. I overreacted, however just briefly, until I swam free from the boat... and afterward... and afterward... I stood up! One of my feet ended up contacting the riverbed and I understood I was remaining in only two feet of water.

I was knee-somewhere down in the Willamette, several feet from the dock where my new paddling mentor Chris Wojda was giggling madly.

"Yes, you're not a rower," he expressed, attempting to quit snickering. "Suppose we attempt once more?"

Admission: I'd never been in a skiff prior to focusing on paddling across the Drake Passage. I'd never gone drifting at day camp, never fished from the center of a mountain lake, never at any point sat with a young lady on one of those "Passage of Love" rides at an event congregation. About the nearest I'd come was a paddling machine at the exercise center. No inquiry, turning into the first to cross the Drake in a paddle boat was crazy — but I was right here.

That's right — me, the person who'd simply fallen hard into two feet of water. The person who lacked the ability to take a full stroke on this first pass. It was embarrassing, dampening, disappointing... yet, hello, it probably been damn interesting to a person like Chris.

Turned out it was likewise damn entertaining to this sweet-appearing to be more seasoned lady in an uproarious sun cap, who incidentally turned out to be on the waterway in her own single scull. She streaked me a fake approval as she passed. "Quite harsh over here today, huh?" she said with a laugh.

In truth, the water was quiet — not exactly like a shiny lake at sunrise before the breeze can unsettle the surface, however close. So in addition to the fact that i was left considering what had compelled me figure I could take on this beyond ridiculous Drake Passage venture, however I currently needed to experience the outrage of being prodded by an outsider.

I didn't see myself as a rower — yet — as well as the possibility of placing myself in an outrageous climate and battling my direction over, around, or through it held colossal allure. So I got at it before I was well and really prepared, which made sense of how I'd come to humiliate myself in this manner under the careful focus of a person I'd quite recently enlisted to take care of me.

About that. I'd contacted Chris simply the prior week. He was a neighborhood paddling mentor, and we shared a few companions practically speaking, so I fixed him as somebody who could perhaps assist with raising me to an acceptable level. I requested that he lunch, let him know I had a task I needed to examine. He was at that point situated when I showed up, at a road side bistro in Portland, only a couple of blocks from the primary house I resided in as a youngster. He remained to welcome me.

"Take a gander at you!" I said, as he spread out his six-foot-eight casing and enveloped me by a huge squeeze. I'd failed to remember how tall he was. "What are they taking care of you?"

He giggled — a full-throated, full-bodied chuckle that would before long turn out to be excessively natural. "Haven't seen you since your independent Antarctica crossing, Colin," he said. "Astounding stuff, man. I followed the entire thing."

"Much appreciated, Chris," I said. "Implies a great deal. In all honesty, I'm gone to Antarctica again in a couple of months. That is the very thing I needed to converse with you about."

We put down.

"Antarctica, huh?" he said. "The call of nature."

"In addition to that," I said. "This time, I'm going there in a paddle boat, across the Drake Passage."

Chris gave me a confounded look — one that appeared to say, Who in the world is this person, figuring he can line to Antarctica?

I filled him in. I educated him concerning the undertaking, which was planned to start in 90 days, transferred how I'd gotten Discovery to create a full length narrative of the intersection called The Impossible Row, and depicted different rowers I'd collaborate with on the excursion.

"Amazing," Chris said, after I'd spread it out for him. "Want to say I was envious, yet don't realize that I'd be up for an excursion like that. Sea paddling is intense, man. Educate me concerning the boat. Might it be said that you are clear paddling or sculling?"

To Chris, this was a basic inquiry, such as inquiring as to whether I was left-given or right-gave.

As far as I might be concerned, he should have been requesting that I split the molecule.

"Uh," I said, "what's the distinction?"

He saw me like I'd gone distraught. "You must be joking?" he said. "You're going to do this crazy thing in only three months."

"That is really why I called you," I said. "I'm not a rower... yet. I want assistance."

Chris calmly made sense of how clear paddling was the point at which the rower has two hands on a solitary paddle — like you see in university paddling in an eight-man boat. In sculling, the rower holds one paddle in each hand and is answerable for fueling the two sides of the boat.

"That one," I said timidly, without a ton of trust in my response. "I believe it's just one."

Once more, Chris saw me like I two or three screws free, and for an abnormal second he said nothing — he only sort of gazed at me. I think he understood what I was going to request from him, and he was attempting to sort me out.

I moved to fill the quiet. I said, "90 days isn't the issue. I should meet the remainder of the team in Scotland in three weeks for a test column to start preparing as a unit. The Discovery creation group will be there, and I would rather not embarrass myself."

"Three weeks?" he asked, with a baffled look. "That is not much of time."

"Enlighten me," I said.

Then, Chris sensibly inquired as to whether I'd been doing anything by any means to prepare for this excursion, so I let him know I was back working out with my dear companion and mentor Mike McCastle.

"You recollect my solidarity mentor, Mike?" I inquired.

Chris gestured. That's what I knew whether he'd been following my performance journey through the frozen landmass, he was likely mindful of the insane Mr. Miyagi-type exercises Mike had concocted to set me up for the super polar circumstances I'd look on the ice — yet to be certain I taken out my telephone and lined up a video from my Instagram feed.

The majority of individuals who followed me via virtual entertainment knew Mike McCastle resembled a sibling to me. He was persevering — as a mentor as well as a card-conveying boss by his own doing. He'd held the world record for most draw ups in 24 hours — 5,804, crushing the sign of 4,030 set by another notable boss, the ultramarathoner and resigned Navy SEAL David Goggins. Mike had pulled a 2.6-ton Ford F-150 for 22 miles across Death Valley, quite possibly of the most smoking put on Earth, flipped a 250-pound truck tire the distance of a half-long distance race, and climbed a rope what might be compared to Mount Everest in a little more than 24 hours.

A portion of his preparation techniques were insidious, however they were motivated, and compelling as damnation. I entrusted him with my life… and athletic profession.

"Here," I said, giving Chris the telephone. "Look at this."

In the video, Mike was having me do boards with my hands in ice containers, and afterward a progression of squats with my feet in ice while taking care of a lot of Lego issues with my frozen fingers to keep my brain and smoothness sharp.

"Could appear to be odd," I cleared up for Chris, describing as he watched, "yet these reproductions Mike made in the rec center in a real sense saved my life when I was distant from everyone else in Antarctica. We were unable to go to Antarctica to prepare, so Mike brought Antarctica here."

"That is perfect. Mike is fantastic, love him," Chris said as he gave back my telephone, "however what might be said about the Drake? Those waters are terrible and cold and deceptive. No chance he can recreate that here in Portland."

"Try not to be so certain," I said. "Mike is a few bricks short of a load this one. Only a few days ago, he hauled me up at two a.m. Jenna was in on it, she'd given him a key, and he was right there, shaking me conscious, remaining over me out of the loop. I assumed I was having a terrible dream, yet he yelled at me to get my butt up and get to work."

I let Chris know how I was still drowsy, half-utterly crazy when Mike hauled me outside and put me through another of his wild exercises — this one intended to mimic a mad, enraged (and freezing!) sea crossing. He'd set up four Bosu balls, onto which he'd adjusted a standard paddling machine, so the device was shaking and influencing in manners I could anticipate in those violent waters. As I paddled, he continued to soak me with pails of ice water at sporadic stretches, the water consuming my face and slapping me conscious; the entire time he was peppering me with essential math and recent developments inquiries to ensure I was focused intellectually as well as genuinely.

In his own specific manner, Mike was trying my responsibility, my boldness, my lucidity of vision to stand up to the difficulties I'd look in probably the most undermining waters on Earth.

Chris didn't appear to be persuaded that a progression of creative exercises could get me where I should have been for this undertaking — or transform me into a rower. It was anything but an add-water-and-mix sort of arrangement. He was on the right track to have one or two doubts: I was absolutely not a rower, despite the fact that I had good expectations about gathering this test.

Chris probably detected my assurance as I discussed the task over lunch, be that as it may, in light of the fact that he consented to work with me. The more we visited, the more his disposition appeared to mellow. What went over, I think, was that I'm most agreeable external my usual range of familiarity. That is where I really focus on. I'm attracted not exclusively to doing things that have never been finished, yet to doing things I've never finished.

"I understand what you're able to do, Colin," Chris at last said, "so this isn't absolutely insane. Be that as it may, I've been paddling for more than a quarter century, I actually have a long way to go. I'd be stressed assuming it was me intending to do this line. However, I can perhaps show you a couple of things, establish some groundwork."

I hopped up from the table in energy. Truly, I was so totally siphoned he was ready to help me, so appreciative.

Chris expressed that in the brief time frame we had we could chip away at my stance, my timing, and my muscle memory. That's what he felt if I would streak train my body to work the paddles to accuracy, I'd essentially have the option to fall into musicality with different rowers and figure out how to ride out.

"Meet me at the dock Monday morning," he said. "Five a.m. sharp. We'll see what you have and begin there."

So that makes sense of how I came to be remaining in knee-profound water on this peaceful stretch of the Willamette River, humiliated, two or three feet from the dock, while Chris looked on, his monster outline bent over in giggling as I beat the surface in disappointment.

I felt like a misrepresentation — the banner kid for an inability to embrace success. I wasn't accustomed to broadcasting my naiveté in such a public manner, however I was right here, with no great explanation to think I got an opportunity of pulling this off.

One thing it would have assisted with knowing was that these smooth one-man sculls were flimsy as damnation. You needed to sort of lash your feet into the paddling station while some way or another keeping the boat in balance — just, as I'd quite recently taken in the most difficult way possible, on the off chance that you let go of one of the paddles to go after your feet, say, the vessel would move with you.

"You must plume the cutting edges!" Chris hollered at me from the harbor, motioning me to turn the paddle edges lined up with the water for strength, as I attempted to get back in the boat and self-right. "Paddling 101. Never let go of the paddles."

Thus, I padded the paddles, very much like he'd illustrated.

I went after the foot lashes and enclosed my feet back by the Velcro ties — one hand on the paddles, one hand working the ties.

The boat shook and wobbled as I inclined forward and attempted to keep up with my equilibrium, thinking, This crap is way harder than it looks.

I took a full breath and ready to take off, wanting to think not to humiliate myself a second time in these nothing waters.

"Alright," Chris hollered. "At the point when the boat is steady, square the cutting edges and take a stroke."

Cutting edges in… arms connected with… legs pushing.

I took my most memorable stroke, and afterward a second. By the third stroke, the dock had begun to retreat into the distance, and when I saw that I'd gone around fifty feet, I let out a victorious cry.

"I'm a rower!" I shouted. "I'm a rower!"

Obviously, I was nothing of the sort, yet I was coming.

HOW THIS STORY APPLIES TO YOU

When you search in the mirror, do you see yourself just as you are? Or on the other hand do you additionally see the individual you'll turn into?

Having the option to see the individual I'd become was the means by which I had the option to take the jump from never having paddled a boat to paddling the Drake Passage.

How I arrived was by having a significant impact on from a proper outlook to a development mentality — ideas started by Stanford brain research teacher Carol Dweck. I went from figuring as far as how I can't treat what I can do.

According to a decent outlook, "I'm this individual at this time, and I'll be nothing unique." You let yourself know you're great at math however not extremely inventive — or that you have an ear for music yet not so much for dialects. It's what it is, and you are what your identity is... end of conversation. These decent ideas become a piece of your character, so that you're not liable to develop or change or take a stab at a genuinely new thing.

According to a development outlook, "I might be this one individual at this time, however there's not a great explanation I can't develop, develop, and figure out how to be some other kind of individual in the following second." It's that through difficult work and assurance, you can learn and get to the next level.

Embracing a development mentality is an essential part of living with a Possible Mindset.

Let's assume you went to graduate school and have been working at an enormous firm for the beyond twenty years. As of late, you were struck by an incredible business thought. However at that point your proper mentality kicked in. I'm not a business visionary. I'm a legal counselor. I bill hours, that is my specialty. Help me out. Battle that inclination. Certainly, you're not a business visionary presently, yet there's no great explanation you can't become one. Permit your development attitude to claim this new character, and simply start the cycle.

We as a whole need to begin some place, isn't that so?

Consider it: everyone who has had an effect in their field began from a position of naiveté. Kobe Bryant couldn't ever have changed the scene of ball in the event that he hadn't stepped on the court one day as a youngster and made his most memorable effort. Janis Joplin wasn't an age characterizing performer until she got a guitar and played her most memorable harmonies. Meryl Streep wasn't an entertainer until she tried out for her most memorable school play. Stephen King needed to plunk down and compose the primary sentence of his most memorable book before he could compose his sixty-fourth book. These game-changing specialists and competitors didn't hold on until they were at the highest point of their fields to claim that piece of their personality. They just awakened one day and started the cycle.

Today can be that day for you. This. Very. Day. Let's assume it without holding back:

I'm a b-ball player!

I'm a performer!

I'm an entertainer!

I'm an essayist!

I'm a rower!

Anything that decent picture of yourself you're conveying, put it away. Guarantee your new character. Record it here.

I'm a _____.

(Truly, snatch a pen and record it on paper. Go for it. I'll stand by.)

Make it a piece of your life. For hell's sake, put it in your virtual entertainment profile, assuming that is the stuff to get your head around the thought. Anything it is you need to be or do or attempt, give it voice. Make progress toward it. Own it. Incorporate it. Really impact your outlook and accomplish anything. Realize that anything it is you don't have the foggiest idea how to do, you can figure out how to do. (Hello, that is what Google is really going after?)

Additionally, realize that you could stagger now and again as you find your direction, very much as I did when I flipped over on that shallow stretch of the waterway. That is important for the arrangement. Plan for it. Furthermore, tell yourself before you stumble into the stream that when you do, you'll pick yourself right back up and get right back at it. Realize that these underlying battles are the keys to development and learning... they're not disappointments. The main disappointment is in not attempting.

One of the apprehensions that holds a large number of us back from getting out of our paths is that we could feel as we don't have a place, or that individuals around us are more grounded, more astute, or better. An inability to embrace success is a genuine article. I realize I've felt it on many events — in addition to that morning on the Willamette River.

You've likely experienced it on the main day of a new position, or perhaps at an evening gathering with a lot of individuals you don't actually have the foggiest idea who appear to be far more effective — that feeling that you don't exactly fit in or that you're some way or another not commendable. However, attempt to recollect that everyone at your new position most likely had similar first-day nerves. Those way more "effective" people situated around the supper table — they've all felt overpowered or overmatched at one time, until finding their direction. The way in to their prosperity isn't some huge mystery, it's very basic: those individuals gobbling and energetically trading stories awakened one day and had the certainty to accept they could develop and advance into individuals they've become. You're not a faker, you do have a place.

So go on, thoroughly search in the mirror and see the individual you desire to be, guarantee your personality. Turn into the individual you desire to be. Today.

KEY TAKEAWAY

You are a rower (or anything you desire to be)

Quit letting yourself know that you're not this or you can't do that. That is only your decent attitude talking. The way to opening your fullest potential is to embrace a development mentality. There's nothing that you can't be, you can do anything. Quit thoroughly searching in the mirror and being disheartened with who you are correct now, and begin finding in your appearance the boundless conceivable outcomes of who you can turn into.

HOW THIS APPLIES TO YOUR 12-HOUR WALK

Probable, you've never strolled twelve hours in a single day. This will be new. At the ongoing second you're not a "12-Hour Walk finisher." By embracing a development mentality, you'll understand you're fit for completing this new test. Whenever you've finished the 12-Hour Walk, you'll have demonstrated to yourself that having a development outlook in all components of your life will permit you to be and become anything you focused on.

WITH A POSSIBLE MINDSET,

I can learn, develop, and become anything.

CHAPTER FIVE

Restricting BELIEF: "I'M BROKEN AND WILL NEVER BE THE SAME."

Liberate yourselves from mental subjugation, none however ourselves can free our psyches.

—Bounce MARLEY

"Make it stop!" I shouted. "If it's not too much trouble, make it fucking stop!"

I'd never envisioned such agony was conceivable — the sort of aggravation you'd expect in a dungeon, on a combat zone, or in a trimming tool slaughter... not in a clinic.

The lower half of my body had been totally scorched, and it seemed to me like my legs were still ablaze, similar to I was being wounded by hot blades, similar to there were bugs creeping all around my skin. I'd experienced such serious second-and severe singeing that my sensitive spots were totally uncovered — and now that my aggravation prescriptions had been ceased, I was in outright anguish.

I didn't know I trusted in that frame of mind, He was right here — in my requests, in my desolate weeps for help, all over.

"Satisfy God, make it stop! Fucking damnation!"

My mom had flown most of the way all over the planet to be next to me and love me through these terrible minutes, yet even she was unable to occupy the spaces where the aggravation prescriptions had been.

"Colin," she said, her seat pulled near me in my emergency clinic bed. "I don't have the foggiest idea what to do. Let me know how I can help you."

Her attitude was quiet, yet I could see she was attempting to maintain a reasonable level of control for me. Inside, I knew, she was panicked, shattered, however she would have rather not allowed it to show.

"Make it stop," I cried. "Inspire them to give me something to make it stop." I was crying, shouting, wriggling in distress. There was no limit to it.

I was lying on my back in a Thai emergency clinic, in a coarse paper medical clinic outfit, my legs thickly swathed from my toes to my midsection, however not so thickly wrapped that I was unable to see the blood and puss leaking through the dressing and the tape. It was a ghastliness show. I was unable to look... I was unable to not look. My legs were in a half leg lift, suspended in midair — the best way to get even the littlest piece of help from my own extra weight pushing down on those open nerves.

I'd recently been moved from a no frills neighborhood emergency clinic on the island of Koh Samui, in the Gulf of Thailand, where the paint on the walls was chipped and stripping, where a wild looking feline moved across my bed in what passed for the ICU, where a specialist came to inspect me four days into my difficulty and reported in broken English that I'd at no point ever walk typically in the future.

Prior that day, as I was being stacked into a clinical vehicle plane, a medical caretaker had come and yanked the fentanyl dribble from my arm. I was excessively out of it to scrutinize her. My mother was giving her all to deal with my change to Bangkok's greater medical clinic and made some noise.

"Hello," she yelled, defensive of my consideration, "he wants those drugs!"

"The drug," the attendant expressed, "it's for here." And with that she strolled back to her vehicle on the landing area of the little island's air terminal.

My mother stared at me as she sat alongside my cot toward the rear of the confined plane. We were both befuddled and overpowered by all that was going on.

The one-hour trip to Bangkok via air rescue vehicle was all my desolated body could deal with. I was unable to remain in that medical clinic on Koh Samui, yet I was unable to go the distance. It was absolutely impossible that I could travel as far as possible home to the USA in my delicate state, so it was concurred that I'd face this conflict in Thailand. Tragically, when we showed up at the more current emergency clinic in Bangkok, I was staggering, my agony medications presently completely worn off. The attendant doing my admission made sense of that she couldn't simply shoot me up with a full portion of extraordinary narcotics, what's more it was the late evening and the drug specialist wouldn't return until 8 a.m.

"A lot of medication," she said, making an honest effort to speak with me in English. "To an extreme, once. To an extreme, hazardous. You have stand by till morning."

My mom sat by the bed in my new clinic room and attempted to divert me from the aggravation. She was radiant, and confident, in spite of the fact that I understood later that she didn't believe I should perceive how totally went crazy she truly was. At the time, it probably been anguishing so that her might see her kid experience along these lines, yet she attempted to cheer me up in the ways she could.

As a cheerful interruption, she began enlightening me for the millionth time concerning the tune that she had replayed over and over when she brought forth me at home on a hippy community 22 years sooner — Bob Marley's "Reclamation Song."

"That tune helped me through," she said.

It was the last tune Bob Marley recorded before he kicked the bucket, and the principal melody I heard as I appeared on the scene.

I'd constantly adored this story, however seconds ago I didn't have the persistence for it. There was no diverting me from the pounding, stinging, consuming sensation in my legs — that is, until my mom began singing this heart-lifting, heart-recuperating tune of opportunity that was as much a piece of me as air. The singing was something to occupy us, she let me know later, a spot to invest her effort, her inclination.

Several sections, I participated, as loud as possible:

"Reclamation Songs! These tunes of opportunity!"

For my purposes, it was a spot to put my torment — a method for venturing from the damnation I was in and into a more quiet state.

Again and again, we sang that melody — increasingly loud each break. The way to my room was open, on the grounds that my mom had figured it could get a fire going in the staff in the event that they could hear my shouts, however now that we'd began diverting Bob Marley, I was unable to think about the thing these individuals were thinking. We were singing, shouting at the highest points of our lungs — for right around eight hours! Notwithstanding myself, regardless of my torture, I'd passed into a practically trancelike express, a contemplation... until at last, kindly, I fell into a profound rest.

Eight days sooner, I'd been on an ocean side in the Gulf of Thailand with my closest companion David Boyer. It was mid 2008 and we on was intended to be the postcollege excursion that could only be described as epic — and it was, it ended up, yet not in the ways we'd envisioned. We were all over town one night when we saw a blazing leap rope presentation down the ocean side from where we were remaining.

Moronically, I participated, and in a brief moment my life changed. I got tangled in the fire rope and was promptly overwhelmed on fire. In a frenzy, I wrestled liberated from the blazing rope, which had been splashed in lamp fuel, and naturally ran into the sea to stifle the flares, where I felt a glimmer of help. Getting out of the surf, I peered down at my body to see enormous areas of skin hanging off me like roasted backdrop in a censured house.

Some way or another, David got me to a stopgap facility — down a soil way on a sulked! After I was moved to the more present day clinic in Bangkok, I remained on for north of a month, until the specialists said it was ok for me to travel. In all that time, my mom remained close by — nursing me, adoring me, cajoling me through this terrible experience. It was godlike, truly, the manner in which she held tight with me.

Every day, my mom sat with me and supported for myself and attempted to cheer me up. On one occasion she went to me and said, "Colin, we should define an objective." Her brightness and energy were all the while radiating through.

I pushed back, inquiring, "What objective? I simply need my life back."

She expressed, "Come on, a genuine objective. A substantial objective. The specialist says you'll at no point ever stroll in the future regularly.

Let me know how you'll defy expectations. Help me out, shut your eyes and picture something positive."

I at last viewed her idea in a serious way, and I shut my eyes and thought about it. Without precedent for quite a while, I grinned.

She saw my demeanor change and said, "What? What do you see?"

I shut my eyes, and some place in the fever of my brain I could picture a waterway, a bicycle, a long and winding street. I said, "I see myself crossing the end goal of a marathon."

To her extraordinary and never-ending credit, my mom didn't snicker or advise me to picture a more practical dream. She just embraced me and grinned and said she'd assist with getting that going.

Convinced by my mother to concoct an objective, I had attempted to picture the best version of myself, thus I recalled when I was a youngster, watching the Kona Ironman Triathlon on TV interestingly. I hadn't understood it was a firmly established want of mine to cross a marathon finish line, however it was right here. All it took was putting the desire out there and giving it voice to cause it to appear to be conceivable.

A month or so later, I was at last set free from that Bangkok emergency clinic and cleared to fly home. I was continued and off a progression of planes and pushed around in a wheelchair. My legs were vigorously wrapped. I actually hadn't made a solitary stride.

The day after I got back to Portland, I sat with my mom in the kitchen, in the house in which I'd grown up, not yet understanding that this would be the day the remainder of my life would begin. Consistently, my mom and I had discussed my objective of finishing a marathon. We'd held the possibility out before us like a carrot — or all the more precisely, a help. Yet, on this day, my mom pushed me to activity. She sat opposite me and said, "Today, you want to venture out."

She pulled a wooden seat from our kitchen table and set it out before me in my wheelchair and said, "Today, you will escape that seat and step over to this one."

I peered down at the wrap on my legs and saw the blood and scabs through the bandage and tape. I realized my legs had started to decay underneath those wrappings — crap, they were no greater than my arms! The bulk I'd spent a lifetime building had evaporated. The new skin coming in at my knee and lower leg joints was tight to the point that I had practically zero portability, so I realized it would take all of battle I could bring to make that one stride.

I sat in my wheelchair for three hours prior to marshaling the boldness to venture out and remained on my rankled and swathed feet prior to falling again into the wooden seat.

However, my mother didn't allow me to stop. She continued to push me. The following day she moved the seat five stages away, the following day ten.

It was an exhausting movement, however a movement, regardless. With each step I was willing myself entirety. Inconvenience was, I was all the while living in my mom's storm cellar, actually hearing those dismal words from the Thai specialist who'd basically let me know my life was finished.

You won't ever walk regularly from now onward.

Up until this point, he was correct — and notwithstanding my having the option to limp around for brief periods, I was feeling discouraged and abandoned. It had been very nearly a long time since I'd moved on from school. Everybody I'd gone to class with was out there on the planet, making commotion, working, living all alone, and I realized I expected to move on.

I began going after positions. My uncle Neal assisted me with handling my most memorable genuine meeting, at a wares exchanging firm Chicago. The organization flew me in to meet with the proprietor. I ventured warily into the lift of their midtown place of business and squeezing the button for one of the upper floors — the 44th, I think. I was separated from everyone else. I got a brief look at myself in the lift reflect. I was dressed to dazzle: a fresh, white-caught shirt; a tie my mom assisted me with choosing; an impeccably squeezed sets of jeans. I gave myself a quick overview, from head to toe, it was all set to ensure I. Shirt: check. Pants: check. Certainty: check.

However at that point as my eyes dropped, I saw I was wearing a couple of cushy room shoes. My heart sank... and my certainty fell right alongside it. I thought, Oh, definitely those. My feet were as yet screwed up. I'd been charred, couldn't wear shoes. That made sense of the shoes, which had become such a reality of my new life that I'd come to acknowledge them. They were a piece of me. Inconvenience was, in the wellbeing of my own home, I never needed to think what they looked like. Around here in reality, they didn't precisely establish the right vibe.

I was unable no doubt, however it seemed to me like the secretary was taking a gander at me entertaining when I ventured off the lift. You know that inclination, when you understand you have a piece of food caught in your teeth and can't help thinking about what number of individuals you've cooperated with since you last ate? You're embarrassed, yet you're not exactly certain how humiliated? I was at that point hesitant about strolling with a limp and a dubious walk, and presently it was soaking in that I'd dressed for a big deal frame new employee screening as though I were hitting up a sleep party.

I moved toward the secretary and gave my name. She let me know somebody would be on a mission to see me not long from now and guided me to a seat in the holding up region.

"Anything I can get you?" she asked as I backed away from her work area. "Water? Espresso? A cool refreshment?" A couple of shoes? I envisioned her asking straightaway.

All things considered, I understood she was basically broadening an office generosity — a standard demonstration of neighborliness she'd have offered any guest. At that point, in any case, it felt to me as though she saw me as delicate — that my shoes flagged I was frail or off or not exactly. What's more, as those restless minutes in the banquet room ticked by, I went from accepting I was prepared to expert this meeting to thinking I wasn't prepared in any way.

I attempted to chill out. Obviously, when the CEO ventured out to welcome me, he saw my feet immediately. He was a major, tall person, with a strut I'd come to connect with a large number of the influencers in the structure. He let out a little grin — a look a greater amount of bemusement than entertainment.

A voice inside my head said, So much for dressing to intrigue, Colin.

He demonstrated my feet with an unobtrusive gesture and said, "Shoes?"

I was embarrassed, that this was the initial feeling I'd made, however I attempted to disregard it. I'd come this far, I thought. I wasn't going to let a couple of fluffy room shoes hold me back from starting the remainder of my life.

"It's a boring tale," I said.

I shared the boring tale in the meeting, and a couple of different things other than — and I wound up landing the position. Furthermore, when I moved to Chicago a brief time frame later, I fell into an everyday practice. Every day, I figured out how to walk a little farther, in somewhat less aggravation. I was not even close to where I needed to be, however I would shed my shoes soon enough and make a tolerable showing of appearing "ordinary."

When I began work, I'd moved on from shoes to appropriate dress shoes.

At some point, when the majority of my partners had called it a day, I arrived at under my work area for a sack containing tennis shoes. I was spotted by John, whose work area was close to mine. We were around a similar age, yet he'd been at the firm longer. He'd began his profession the second he graduated school. We both authoritatively answered to senior administration, however he was my true chief. As he put on his jacket and scarf, he saw me getting out of my dress shoes and into my new running shoes. He got my attention and said, "Today's really frightful out there. Wrap up."

"Definitely," I said, rapidly moving to leave the workplace.

"What's with the tennis shoes, Colin?" he inquired.

"I'm preparing for a marathon," I said, similar to it was the most regular thing on the planet.

"Pause, what?" he shot back. "I see you consistently, and you can scarcely walk."

I grinned, peering down at my running shoes. "As a matter of fact, to kick off my preparation, I've focused on strolling to and from work."

"So you're going to head back home?" John asked, distrustful.

"Consistently," I said gladly.

John knew where I resided — about a half-hour stroll from downtown. "Are you utterly insane?" he inquired. "It's seven degrees Fahrenheit out there. The breeze is whipping off the lake. No one strolls around Chicago around mid-

"No one except for me," I expressed, binding up my shoes. What's more, with that, I limited off into the Windy City evening, prepared to take on the world... mindfully.

The kicker to this story is that mid year I came to the beginning line of the Chicago Triathlon. I arrived by degrees, and by plan. In the wake of banking that large number of miles strolling to and fro to work, I joined an exercise center not excessively far from my office. I swam in the pool. I rode the exercise bike. At last, I began running on the treadmill. I was ghastly scared of falling in the city of Chicago in winter and scraping up my legs before they got an opportunity to recuperate, so I did the vast majority of my preparation inside. Every day I did somewhat more... until I was at last ready to move toward the beginning line upon the arrival of the race and plunge into Lake Michigan and swim my most memorable mile.

I didn't simply finish the race as I'd trusted, yet by some sweet combination of coarseness and self control I won, putting first generally in a field of more than 4,000. Yet, the genuine triumph for me was simply being there, eighteen months in the wake of shutting my eyes and envisioning myself at that time.

I'd set the race out before me like an unrealistic fantasy and figured out how to make that little glimpse of heaven.

HOW THIS STORY APPLIES TO YOU

Regardless of how you've been broken, you have the ability to fabricate yourself back up. Assuming you're powerless, you can make areas of strength for yourself. Assuming you're broken, you can assemble yourself back. Assuming you're injured, realize that you can mend.

I wouldn't be where I am today in the event that my mom hadn't trained me to lay out an objective for myself in that Bangkok clinic room. An illustration that would turn into a center fundamental of the Possible Mindset.

I could never have taken on any of the out there or unimaginable tasks that have characterized my life since winning that marathon.

I wouldn't compose this book... no doubt.

In any case, that is the thing about objectives. Practical, apparently unreasonable — it doesn't make any difference. At the point when you imagine what you need to achieve, when you give it voice and organization, you start zeroing in on the positive prospects as a whole. Furthermore, when you're broken in how I was broken, when you've been informed that your life won't ever from now onward be something similar, you can either acknowledge your destiny or battle like damnation to recover what you've lost — perhaps arrive at a superior spot.

On the size of 1 to 10 I expounded on before, my consume mishap was a 1. It hurt. It sucked. It caused a lot of individuals a lot of aggravation... not simply me. In any case, there's no rejecting that it made a way for this large number of 10s that followed. It constrained me to zero in on what I truly desired, and the difficult work important to arrive.

So feel free to make the way for the 10s that are ready to be found. Assuming that right currently you're attempting to put stock in yourself, know this: I trust in you.

How about we venture out toward your seat together. Very much as I did in that Thai emergency clinic envisioning myself crossing a marathon finish line, assuming you feel broken, I believe you should shut your eyes and picture yourself entirety. What do you see? What's going on with you? How can it feel? Clutch that vision and keep it sharp to you.

Now that you've characterized your major objective, your Everest, you'll perceive how basically having it can speed you not too far off to recuperation. You realize I love major objectives, yet in this exercise major objectives can be a snare since they frequently feel such a long ways too far that we don't have any idea where to start.

This is where the following stage becomes possibly the most important factor. The main step.

Ask yourself: What single gradual step might I at any point take today to draw me one stage nearer to that major objective? What little forward-moving step is reachable? No step is excessively little.

What is your "wheelchair to the wooden seat" second? Make that stride, and afterward push the seat farther away tomorrow. Focus on moving forward every day, and you'll be astounded at how rapidly you'll trade your shoes for tennis shoes, prepared to cross your "marathon finish line" in a flash.

No inquiry, there are wounds, handicaps, and sicknesses that deny us the opportunity to at any point be something similar — and there's no piece of hard-won exhortation or persuasive procedure I can share to turn around that sort of situation. But I'm continually motivated by accounts of individuals conquering goliath snags and pushing themselves ahead. The one who was deadened in a mishap however proceeded to turn into a productive craftsman utilizing his mouth to paint. The one who was brought into the world without legs, yet at the same time proceeded to win sixteen gold decorations at the Paralympic Games. The deep rooted skier who extinguished her knees and took up whitewater kayaking as a better approach to propel herself. They all show us the force of the human soul; each advises us that our capability to flourish is boundless with the right outlook.

Assuming that you've at any point broken a bone or confronted an overwhelming system like a knee substitution medical procedure, you've presumably heard an orthopedist say that when the bone mends it'll be more grounded than at any other time, or on the other hand, that the man-made parts in your new knee will be more sturdy than the natural parts at any point were.

A similar applies to anything it is you're confronting: You'll be more grounded tomorrow than you are today. You'll be more proficient tomorrow than you are today. Perhaps not in the same ways you were areas of strength for once skilled, yet in every one of the ways that matter.

The narrative of my consume injury is an example in the force of steady objective setting, but on the other hand it's an illustration in steadiness and coarseness and positive reasoning — which are all urgent parts of a Possible Mindset. I'm the same as you. In the event that I can do whatever it may take, so can you. We as a whole have the ability to move our outlook toward the positive and envision a more promising time to come.

Feel free to reach. Push forward. Assemble yourself back.

KEY TAKEAWAY

Trade your shoes for tennis shoes

You may be harmed. You may be managing a misfortune and contemplating whether you'll at any point be something very similar. Or on the other hand you may be disappointed that at a past time in your life you were more grounded. This present circumstance doesn't need to be super durable. Keep in mind, I set all my worldwide bests after I was broken. You, as well, have the ability to modify yourself. Put forth a gradual objective. Make your most memorable strides. Trade out your shoes for tennis shoes.

HOW THIS APPLIES TO YOUR 12-HOUR WALK

Comprehend, the 12-Hour Walk isn't simply a practice in actual perseverance. It's not even for the most part a practice in actual perseverance. There's no award for going farther or quicker. The 12-Hour Walk is tied in with preparing your brain. In the event that you can make it around the block once in light of the fact that your knee is woofing, fine. Dial back, have some time off. Harming yourself isn't the objective. You can in any case log your twelve hours by sitting alone with your viewpoints, with no external interruptions. The psychological strength you'll acquire from this challenge will move you no less than one bit nearer to conquering your ongoing actual difficulties.

WITH A POSSIBLE MINDSET,

I can mend, regardless of whether I've been broken. I can bear backing up, regardless of whether I've been wrecked.

CHAPTER SIX

RESTRICTING BELIEF: "I'M AFRAID OF WHAT PEOPLE WILL SAY."

Analysis is something we can abstain from effectively by saying nothing, sitting idle, and being nothing.

—ARISTOTLE

"I believe I will leave my place of employment," I said into my telephone.

Quietness.

"Grandmother Sue, would you say you are there?"

"Indeed, I'm here," she said. "I'm simply attempting to consider a more unpretentious method for saying this, yet I'm coming up clear, so it is right here. That is a horrible thought, Colin."

Then more quietness.

I don't know what I'd been anticipating. Grandmother Sue had been by and large steady of my important choices. She was a pleased, dedicated Chicago local, and had raised my mother and her four kin there. Simply that morning she had been the main individual from my family toward the end goal of the Chicago Triathlon, and she'd taken me to breakfast after the competition to praise my unexpected triumph. But her reaction seconds ago passed on nothing to understanding.

I'd recently wrapped up let my grandmother know how, after she dropped me off at my condo following the race that morning, my companion Jenny Gelber had welcomed me over to her folks' home for a grill. Throughout the span of the night I got to chatting with her dad, Brian Gelber, an unbelievable products dealer. I enlightened him regarding my consume mishap eighteen months sooner, my young life fantasy about contending in the Olympics, and the marathon win that day. He'd proposed to support me to reignite my fantasy and pursue a marathon gold decoration at the Olympics.

I'd made it clear to my grandma that he wasn't offering me a heap of cash, to purchase a couple of boarding passes to races and go through my days preparing. I'd highlighted that this "offer" was in no way like getting drafted by a NBA or NFL group. On the off chance that I acknowledged, my way of life would be making a significant stride back monetarily.

"Colin, it was astounding to observe what you exposed there today, however that was for no particular reason. You're a grown-up now, my dear. You should be reasonable," Grandma Sue said, with a genuine yet reprimanding tone.

"In any case, I've generally longed for being an expert competitor, and perhaps this is my last shot," I argued, attempting to persuade myself as much as her.

"See, as your grandma I've generally attempted to urge you to follow your own way, but on the other hand it's my occupation now and again to educate you. Recall what happened keep going time you elapsed on a protected future and went hiking all over the planet all things considered?" She didn't have to fill in the clear — we as a whole knew the aggravation, and disturbance to the family, my consume injury had caused.

She proceeded, "In addition, what might you tell Uncle Neal? He made some serious things happen to land you that position interview. Accept him as a good example; he's bringing up four extraordinary children here in Chicago, and a profession in finance has given him an extraordinary life. Don't you need something very similar? This moment's not the opportunity to discard everything."

"Better believe it... I hadn't pondered what I'd tell Uncle Neal... ," I said, feeling my past fervor collapse.

"After the entirety of the difficult work and penance you put into procuring your financial matters degree, now is the right time to quit messing about and put your schooling to utilize. You have a splendid future in front of you," she expressed, inclining toward what I'd be surrendering with my wildness.

Grandmother Sue was a hard individual to contend with.

"OK, gratitude for talking it over with me," I said, finishing the call soon after.

My marathon gear was tossed on the floor close to the entryway. I threw my telephone on the foot stool and strolled over to get my grimy race garments and flung them into the stacked washer and dryer set settled in the storage room. It was whenever I'd first resided all alone where I didn't need to stroll to the storm cellar with a modest bunch of quarters to do my clothing. It seemed obvious me that my new, prepared to-utilize machines may be an advantage that would disappear in the event that I cast to the side my first "genuine" task to pursue longs for athletic greatness.

I wasn't prepared at this point to drop hustling marathon full-time, so I got my telephone once more and called my companion Eric. As a companion, definitely he'd have a preferred viewpoint on this over my grandmother. We'd been close in school, and after every one of us got occupations in Chicago, we'd been almost indivisible, getting party time after work, remaining out late on ends of the week, watching sports — the normal large city, youthful expert life.

"What's up, man?" I said, then hopped directly into it with no casual banter. "I'm contemplating leaving my place of employment."

"What? Did you get a superior proposal at another exchanging firm or something like that?"

I strolled him through how my day had gone — the marathon win, the sponsorship offer, and my vulnerability about what to do.

"So what is your take?" I asked, completing my clarification.

"Where might you reside? How might everything function?"

"All things considered, this is all new, so I haven't completely sorted it out. Yet, I met an expert long distance runner and previous Olympian named Simon Thompson this end of the week, and he let me know that most folks train in Australia in the cold weather months, you know because it's their mid year so the weather conditions is great for preparing. Simon let me know he'd acquaint me with his mentor in a spot called Canberra in the event that I needed."

"So you will leave your place of employment? Furthermore, move to Australia? Where are you going to reside? Like you'll lease a condo there?"

"I will not have the option to live it up work and furthermore train for the Olympics, so I'll presumably need to move into a common house or track down a lounge chair to rest on for some time. I did something like that when I was going before Thailand — it wasn't downright awful."

"Buddy! I just found out about Canberra. Have you looked this spot into?" I could hear him chuckling while he clicked his console. "It's the capital of Australia, yet it's not even on the coast. I'm perusing a movement gathering called '10 Reasons Why Nobody Should Travel to Canberra.' This spot looks terrible."

As of now I was walking about my condo.

"I haven't found it yet, man. Like I said, it was only one thought." He could see I was getting disappointed with his tone.

"Help me out, Colin. Look outside your window. What do you see?"

"Downtown, uh, the Sears Tower... "

"Truth be told, the Sears fucking Tower! Enormous city, large future," he went on intensely. "You have a wiped out condo, an astonishing position, and we've been smashing it at the bars of late. What more do you need? Try not to leave your place of employment, man. There's such a huge amount for us here. It's just barely the start. Sounds to me like an exemplary instance of the Sunday Scaries. Get some rest. You'll feel better tomorrow."

"You're most likely right. Gratitude for the motivational speech. See you tomorrow for party time."

"G'night, and well done again on the marathon, astounding stuff. Would be cool on the off chance that you won it again the following summer."

I drooped down on my love seat. My body was depleted from the long and extreme day, yet my psyche was all the while dashing. I turned on the TV and flicked through the channels trusting something would catch my consideration. In any case, after around fifteen minutes of channel surfing, I threw the remote, got my keys, and left.

I expected to clear my head, and I thought, perhaps, a night walk would help.

I randomly meandered through the city roads. I could smell the mid year breeze falling off the lake and hear the recognizable sound of the L train skittering down the tracks above. Questions pinged through my psyche: What's the correct way for me? Might I at some point truly relinquish my position and pursue my Olympic dream all things being equal? What'll everybody say assuming I do?

All things considered, I definitely understood what my grandma — and most likely, likewise, my uncle and my companion Eric — would agree. They'll let me know I'm a finished imbecile!

In a little while, I got back to the entryway of my structure and brought a right turn down the lobby past the lift cove to really take a look at my post box prior to tapping out. I put my critical in the lock and tracked down only garbage mail inside.

A more seasoned refined man, most likely in his fifties, with salt-and-pepper hair, strolled into the sorting room all of a sudden. I remembered him from the structure. He was in every case beautifully dressed. We weren't companions, yet I'd traded casual conversation with him in the lift a couple of times, and saw he lived on the highest level.

"Michael, right?" I inquired.

He grinned back and said, "No doubt, great to see you. Did you have a good end of the week?"

Regularly, with a general more odd I'd typically answer with something basic like "Fine" or "Very great" and continue on. We as a whole know that with regards to trading merriments, the individual asking isn't typically searching for the genuine response. Yet, in my confounded state I was unable to help myself, so I dumped a fairly shortened rendition of my end of the week on Michael.

Furthermore, wrapped up with "Thus, I figure I could leave my place of employment and move to Australia. What is your take?"

"Most importantly, congratulations on the marathon, that is a helluva story," he shouted, gesturing, apparently dazzled.

He locked his container, and holding his little pile of mail, he threw his keys in his grasp and suggested a surprising conversation starter back: "Have you seen my vehicle? The Porsche Cayenne?"

"Better believe it, the dark one. I've seen you leave the carport, it's great."

"See, we've all felt the call of experience now and again. I can perceive how in your psyche leaving your place of employment, and moving to another country, looks engaging at present, yet the fact of the matter is, I didn't get to where I am, an extraordinary profession, an agreeable life, by settling on rash choices. My recommendation, since you're asking, is stay with your work, your profession way. Trust me, when you're my age, you'll express gratitude toward yourself for not discarding everything spontaneously."

He gave me a little pat on the shoulder and left my existential emergency as fast as he'd entered it.

I got up the next morning to the recognizable sound of my alert, flawlessly planned so I could execute my standard morning schedule: clean my teeth, shave, shower, get dressed, and walk the thirty minutes to work.

I dodged into the lunchroom and snatched my morning espresso, prior to making a beeline for my work area on the company's exchanging floor. Like normal, I showed up there thirty minutes before the market opened. It was an open floor plan. I had ten screens stacked directly in front of me showing outlines, charts, and various business sectors; they stayed open consistently so I could break down and execute exchanges.

This was my time every morning to find a good pace on the short-term developments in the Asian and European business sectors before the chime rang in New York. In any case, as I opened the news channel on my Bloomberg terminal, I was unable to center.

I brought over to my chief, John, who was situated at the work area to one side. "You got a moment to talk in the gathering room?" I asked.

"Of course, what's happening?"

As we strolled into the gathering room, which comprised of twelve high-upheld cowhide seats and moderate style encompassing a larger than usual focus table, John whirled a pen in his grasp and shut the glass entryway behind me.

"Congrats on the marathon incidentally. A couple of folks from the workplace messaged me about it the previous evening. I can't completely accept that you won. Incredible. You've made considerable progress since you were wearing those shoes," he said, laughing.

I strolled through the rotating entryway and onto the road. As the chill of the morning air hit my cheeks, I thought back up at the glass overshadow, muddled by the fast grouping of occasions. Pressing forward is the only real option now, I thought, cognizant that there'd be a lot more pundits as I depended on my instinct and ventured into my new life.

HOW THIS STORY APPLIES TO YOU

What number of your legends weren't censured en route?

Fair warning: it's a confusing question.

Anybody who's consistently accomplished extraordinary things has been scrutinized by somebody, sooner or later. At the point when you choose to break liberated from the zone of agreeable carelessness to open your best life, make certain to tie on your protection in light of the fact that the pundits are coming.

Have you at any point had an encounter like the accompanying? You post to web-based entertainment about something you're amped up for — say, you're declaring to your local area that you will prepare to run your most memorable long distance race. A few group leave kind and elevating remarks, as:

"Whoopee, well done."

"You will pound it (bicep twist emoticon)."

By the day's end you're looking down your post and see that somebody has left a negative remark, "How could you do that? Appears to be an exercise in futility!"

That evening you battle to nod off as you replay the negative remark in your mind. You carry on to you what you'll tell that individual the following time you see them — to take care of them. Also, in the most pessimistic scenario, you begin to trust the pundit. You ask yourself, Is running an exercise in futility? Would it be a good idea for me not be preparing for the long distance race?

Our ancient cerebrums are designed to be adversely set off by analysis. That is on the grounds that, when we lived in caves, the sensation of disgrace or not having a place was an admonition sign that we wouldn't make due assuming that the clan deserted us. Regardless of this reliance on the gathering done being as outrageous in current life, our DNA actually sets off the survival reaction as a safeguard component to analysis.

The most terrible thing you can do is to attempt to stay away from analysis no matter what while never "trying enormously" to experience your maximum capacity.

As far as I might be concerned, Teddy Roosevelt summarized this best when he said:

Not the pundit counts; not the one who brings up how the resilient man staggers, or where the practitioner of deeds might have improved. The credit has a place with the one who is in the field, whose face is damaged by residue and sweat and blood; who endeavors boldly; who blunders, who comes short over and over... who at the best knows in the end the victory of high accomplishment, and who even from a pessimistic standpoint, on the off chance that he fizzles, essentially falls flat while trying significantly, so his place won't ever be with those cold and shy spirits who neither know triumph nor rout.

Try not to allow one virtual entertainment to remark prevent you from seeking after your objectives. Try not to let the apprehension about what others could say prevent you from pursuing your fantasies, regardless of how senseless or ridiculous they might appear to other people. This is your life, and with a Possible Mindset you have the ability to choose precisely the way in which you need to live it.

I thought let my grandmother know that I quit my place of employment was hard. Years after the fact, I figured out what hard truly was the point at which I began let individuals know that I wanted to stroll across Antarctica alone. Envision the number of forms of "that is a horrendous thought," "don't do that," "it's unthinkable," and "you will fall flat" I heard when I reported that undertaking.

Innumerable. However, that didn't prevent me from attempting.

At the point when I got back from my fruitful performance crossing of Antarctica to worldwide praise, I calmed the pundits who initially let me know it was a poorly conceived notion. Notwithstanding, an altogether new gathering of pundits lifted their hands, expressing belittling things like Colin's intersection was "reachable" and "devised."

You'll once in a while, if at any point, be reprimanded by somebody who's carrying on with their best life. Chances are, those individuals will be aware — and regard — the difficulties of your interest. On a more regular basis, analysis comes from those who're disheartened by the results of their own lives and need an objective for their dissatisfaction and uncertainty.

Is there a general setting to pay attention to valuable analysis, counsel, or criticism? Indeed, totally. The key is figuring out how to recognize helpful analysis from disastrous analysis.

Consider the source.

Assuming that you're being censured by an outsider on the web, that one is simple: disregard it; this individual doesn't really have any acquaintance with you.

On the off chance that you're being censured by a relative, partner, or dear companion, calmly inhale and listen to them. My grandmother, for instance, was really attempting to offer me her best guidance, in light of what she figured my best life ought to seem to be. Frequently, individuals near you can offer significant criticism and a supportive viewpoint. They can try and, similar to a mirror, reflect back to you what you've said you need, and realign you in the event that you're not experiencing your reality. Be that as it may, be mindful so as not to take cues from them aimlessly. For my situation, in choosing to leave my place of employment, I confided in my instinct (we'll go further on instinct soon). Keep in mind, you understand you better than any other person. There are times when you really want to supersede the benevolent analysis of loved ones.

Notwithstanding what you do, individuals will talk — they'll have an assessment on it. You have no control over the thing others will say, just the way in which you respond.

As a matter of fact, I am right here, offering you my best and benevolent guidance on the most proficient method to open your best life. It depends on you to choose if my recommendation merits taking.

Remember: you won't glance back toward the finish of your life and say, "I'm truly happy I kept away from analysis." If you generally twist to the assessments of others, you'll seem to be that delicate elderly person by the lift in the penthouse in Manhattan, thinking about what might have been conceivable if you'd really wanted to experience your reality.

It's not past the point of no return. Try not to allow anybody's analysis to prevent you from entering the field.

KEY TAKEAWAY

Step into the field

At the point when analysis unavoidably comes your direction, pause for a minute to think about its source, and be knowing about whom you decide to pay attention to. Take care of business, make the effort, endeavor boldly, dare significantly in all that you do, and dismiss the "cold and hesitant spirits who neither know triumph nor rout."

HOW THIS APPLIES TO YOUR 12-HOUR WALK

Welcome to the ideal chance to test the strength of your new protection. Probable, when you inform individuals regarding your obligation to finishing the 12-Hour Walk, some will immediately answer with analysis, making statements like "That is a horrendous thought, how could you do that?" Trust that your Walk will prompt fantastic forward leaps. You could try and find that once you're carrying on with your best life, the people who at first scrutinized you will end up enlivened by your change and decide to dare incredibly themselves, endeavoring their own 12-Hour Walk.

WITH A POSSIBLE MINDSET,

I can dare extraordinarily, in any event, while confronting likely analysis.

CHAPTER SEVEN

RESTRICTING BELIEF: "I'M AFRAID OF FAILING."

I've missed in excess of 9,000 shots in my profession. I've lost just about 300 games. multiple times, I've been trusted to make the game-dominating effort and missed. I've bombed again and again in my life. Also, for that reason I succeed.

—MICHAEL JORDAN

It's significant a Brit breaks this excursion first.

Those words reverberated in my mind as I gazed at quite possibly of the most scary man on earth, British Special Forces Captain Louis Rudd.

The smell of flat fly fuel and rust infiltrated my noses. We were packed with many pounds of our singular endurance gear into the rear of a small Twin Otter plane, destined for the external edge of the Antarctic expanse of land where we were going to start a two-month, straight on race across the frozen mainland.

It wasn't simply the plane that was shaking — my certainty was likewise not exactly solid as we moved toward our arrival on the white pit.

There'd been a long heredity of pleased British polar pioneers who'd endeavored different Antarctic undertakings throughout the course of recent years or somewhere in the vicinity. Prior to venturing out from home, Captain Rudd had told a columnist from the Telegraph, "It's significant a Brit breaks this excursion first." He generally assumed it his inheritance to be the Brit who snatched the brilliance of turning into the primary individual to cross the whole body of land of Antarctica solo, unsupported by resupplies, and completely human fueled.

Honestly, he was fundamentally more experienced than I, having finished several noteworthy polar accomplishments as of now — and poop, he was basically what could be compared to a Navy SEAL. Yet, prior to making this excursion to the lower part of the world, I'd gladly told the New York Times how I wanted to sure overcome this apparently "unimaginable first." Now, gazing out at the ice through the window of the plane, and afterward back at Captain Rudd's grizzled face, I wasn't really.

As the plane entryway aired out at my beginning area, the less 25 degree air banged into me like a frozen semitruck. I immediately grabbed up my goggles and facial covering before my skin became streak frozen.

The pilots assisted me with emptying my sled and stuff onto the ice. My heap weighed 375 pounds, loaded with all that I'd have to get by. I'd haul it behind me consistently for the following two months.

"Best of luck," they expressed, moving once more into the cockpit to usher Captain Rudd to his beginning stage.

I'd take all the karma I could get. We'd race almost 1,000 miles to arrive at the opposite side of the landmass. We'd settled on a courteous fellows' consent to begin one pretty far from one another, however equidistant to the main GPS waypoint on the course. The strain was sufficiently high as of now; better we each had our very own piece space to get everything rolling.

The pilots didn't try to take off once more. Rather, I watched the plane taxi over the lopsided landscape, and in a couple of brief minutes the airplane saved Captain Rudd on the ice prior to taking off and passing on us both out there to fight for ourselves.

Antarctica is sweeping indeed. As a mariner encounters crossing an unending sea, you can see white for a significant distance and miles. With clear skies that day, and 24 hours of light in Antarctica that season, Captain Rudd's one-mile cradle didn't seem like a lot. I could nearly make out his sure articulation. I attempted to disregard him while getting together my stuff to start, yet I could feel his presence with each heartbeat.

My fingers were stinging from the cold as I settled the last bits of stuff into my sled and lashed into my saddle interestingly.

I turned on my GoPro to stamp the event. "So at this very moment on November 3, 2018, at 3:22 p.m., I authoritatively start. Starting points are straightforward. You move forward. On the off chance that you're going 1,000 miles or 100 yards, it's something similar," I said into the camera with an apprehensive grin.

My body was fired up like a pure blood's, prepared to detonate from the beginning door. I hurled forward to start and afterward... nothing. I was caught set up.

I shook out my legs and arms like a track star preparing for a race, and attempted once more. A couple of steps this time, and afterward hammer, halted abruptly, incapable to move.

I snorted and moaned. In spite of the fact that I could get my sled rolling for a couple of steps and at one point a couple of moments, I was unable to support the work for a really long time.

I'd realized the sled would be at its heaviest right off the bat — and by straightforward math would gradually get lighter from consuming fuel to dissolve ice into water and from eating food, which basically comprised of hand crafted, entire food, plant-based nourishment bars called "Colin Bars" — however I'd never envisioned that I wouldn't have the option to move my sled by any means.

The sadness started to surpass me like a tempest tide washing over the ocean side.

We as a whole realize despairing people tend to be desperate for kindred spirits, so I looked over at Captain Rudd, hoping to track down him in a similar dilemma. I could never have been all the more off-base. What I saw rather was a tactical man in full walk, gaining consistent headway, apparently with next to no of my equivalent battles.

As I watched him vanish into the great beyond, I remained in a bewildered daze. My eyes liquefied into a stream of tears, filling my goggles. Be that as it may, what happens when it's less 25 degrees outside and you begin crying? The tears stick to your face.

"I'm a woeful disappointment!" I shouted out to the span of Antarctica, tumbling to my knees.

This wasn't my most memorable high-stakes race. My psyche streaked back to a day more than 100 degrees hotter and a world away.

I dove off the barge into the completely clear, blue Caribbean waters of Cozumel, Mexico. Normally you can see for many feet in these serene waters that are widely acclaimed for swimming and scuba plunging. Be that as it may, not today. All things being equal, all I could see was agitated up whitewater. I resembled a wet sock being tumbled in a clothes washer.

I was fighting 65 of the top proficient marathon runners on the planet during the main leg of the Cozumel World Cup, the most recent stop on the International Triathlon circuit. We were all there competing for world-positioning places, wanting to meet all requirements for the Olympics ultimately.

It had been a long time since I'd stop my money work, I was in my fourth season hustling as a genius, and I was respected to address the USA on the world stage. However, after such a long time, I actually hadn't had the breakout execution I expected to genuinely demonstrate I merited one of the sought after Olympic spots.

Perhaps today was that day.

I'd become companions with a large number of the folks as we hustled and went all over the planet for quite a long time at a time following the expert circuit. However when the beginning firearm went off and we dove into the water, there was no space for companionship.

We adjusted the primary turn float, and I stifled on pieces of frothing seawater. Heaving for air, I battled to remain close to the front of the pack, my arms turning like turbines to move me forward. Vast water swimming is nothing similar to the enlightened pool swimming I was familiar with as a university swimmer, where everybody had their own path, and their own space. This was significantly more like a WWE wrestling match.

Notwithstanding the fight in the sea, I attempted to resist the urge to panic while leaving the water. So, all in all started one of the most basic pieces of any marathon race — change.

I ran up the ocean side, proficiently dumping my goggles, cutting on my protective cap, and mounting my bicycle right away, all while running shoeless.

As I jumped onto my bicycle and tied into my bicycle shoes, which were at that point cut to the pedals, I could hear my heart hammering out of my chest. The moist, tropical air filled my lungs and the ninety-degree heat dried the salt water from my skin immediately.

My legs hotly siphoned the pedals as the Mexican fans coating the road applauded us.

"Andale! Andale!" they yelled.

I looked into over my handlebars, checking out my situation in the race interestingly. For hell's sake, yes! I was in an extraordinary position. The words "ESP Gomez" were imprinted on the red race shirt straightforwardly before me.

Javier Gomez of Spain — the dominant World Champion and the London Olympic silver medalist, the demigod of our game — was only a couple of feet ahead.

I'd never been this near the best at this phase of a World Cup. It felt astonishing! I permitted myself a fulfilled grin, feeling without precedent for my expert vocation that I had a place next to the most elite.

I wasn't going to blow this open door. I remained stuck to Gomez's wheel, permitting his slipstream to convey me forward to the front of the race as the miles ticked by. And afterward, Gomez flooded in the last half mile, cementing his situation ahead of the pack before the change to the run. Furthermore, I went with him, matching him pedal for pedal.

I leaped off my bicycle and as my uncovered feet hit the asphalt, I was endlessly neck with the World Champ, heading into the last leg of the race.

We racked our bicycles in the change zone and immediately stuck our feet into our running shoes, enhanced with versatile bands that made fooling around tying them pointless.

Consistently counted.

Step for step, side by side, we ran down the palm tree–lined road. This is all there is to it, Colin, I told myself. Hold tight. Dig profound. You have a place, you can beat him, you will make the Olympics, you have this.

Until I didn't.

Gomez investigated his right shoulder at me, as he changed into another gear. A stuff I didn't have, a stuff obviously saved for the real best, as opposed to a wannabe like me. Furthermore, very much like that, he was no more.

Stay with it, Colin, runner up is as yet a glad completion in a race like this. I stuck to trust. The perspiration flowed down my brow and consumed the edges of my eyes. I attempted each sure self-talk stunt I knew. I asked my legs to fail to remember their aggravation and continue to push.

I broke, and afterward I broke.

Another competitor passed me, and afterward one more and again. I felt like I was moving in reverse. My deepest desires were crashing down. The strength and pride I'd felt minutes before dissipated, supplanted with the queasy sensation of disappointment. I didn't have a place with the best; I wasn't even second best or third best.

As I hauled myself across the end goal, my step seeming to be that of an injured canine than a gazelle, I was in forty-eighth spot.

I found Jenna in the end goal region as the victor, Gomez, and the other two platform finishers commended their prosperity by soaking themselves with containers of champagne.

"I'm never going to make the Olympics, Jenna. I suck. Please accept my apologies you needed to observe that today," I expressed to be honest, attempting to keep down a full scale implosion.

Jenna enveloped me by her arms, not caring that I was absorbing her spotless garments sweat and spit. She rested on her unmistakable confidence, telling me, "Give yourself a little grace, Colin. It's one race. Also, for 66% of it, you looked astounding. You have one more shot one week from now in Puerto Rico. We should get you tidied up."

I wasn't feeling so hopeful, however I faked a grin as we made a beeline for our lodging.

Bang! The beginning firearm went off as we dove into the sea outside Old San Juan, for the following race on the International Triathlon circuit.

I'd made an honest effort to wash off the smell of disappointment from my exhibition the prior week and to start all over again for this race.

I left the water, heart beating again after the unavoidable wrestling match in the ocean, and ran toward my bicycle. The rough cobblestone road sent vibrations through every last trace of my body. I was in the bicycle load with around five different competitors.

"How about we go! We should cooperate," a Guatemalan competitor yelled to our gathering, looking rapidly at me. "We can get the front folks assuming we as a whole work together."

It's standard in a genius bicycle race, whether the Tour de France or an expert draft lawful marathon, to cooperate in a situation like this. On the off chance that each person takes a hard swig at the front, and blocks the breeze until the end of the folks behind him, the aggregate exertion is essentially quicker than going solo.

The five of us immediately conformed. Every last one of us ran at the front for fifteen seconds or somewhere in the vicinity, prior to falling back to the furthest limit of the line, and allowing the following person to proceed. We rode simply creeps off one another's wheels to expand the draft, emulating the controlled mayhem of race vehicle drivers hurdling down the track at the Indy 500.

"We've fucking got this, folks!" I yelled subsequent to taking a turn at the front, an explosion of energy flooding through my legs.

The speed animated. We as a whole stood up out of our bicycle saddles, putting greatest power through our pedals as we advanced out of a clip turn. I was simply in the driver's seat of a Swiss competitor, the momentum head of our gathering, preparing to proceed at the front. He stripped off to one side, and as I felt the additional kind of the breeze hit my body, I turned.

"Shiiiiitttttt!" I hollered.

I was unexpectedly airborne, launched out from my bicycle, similar to Superman without the cape.

I hadn't seen the profound pothole before me soon enough, and presently I was flying through the air, in what felt like sluggish movement, attempting to prepare myself for the unavoidable. While falling I stared at a the observer Puerto Rican banner painted on her cheeks. She lifted her hands to cover her face and wheezed with sickening apprehension at what she was seeing.

Like a baseball player sliding carelessly into home plate, my body scratched across the unpleasant street. Other than my protective cap, I was essentially bare. No gloves, no socks, simply a paper-meager race suit and exposed skin.

Briefly everything was quiet, I was thoroughly numb, and afterward in a hurry, the burning aggravation shot through my body.

"Ambulancia! Ambulancia!" I heard somebody shout.

I moved onto my back and acquired my hands front of my face to overview the harm, flinching in torment. There was no skin on the centers of my hands, simply blood and grime and rock. My race suit was destroyed. Maybe I'd gone heedlessly through a meat processor. Seeing such a lot of skin swinging from my body sent a PTSD shiver through my spirit, taking me back to that Thai clinic years prior.

In a forgiving snapshot of shock, I passed out.

Coming to, I observed that I'd been shipped back to the end goal region and set inside a stopgap clinical tent. I was lying on my back on a table in my very own pool blood.

"Wow. Colin, are you OK?" I heard a voice yell over the clamor of the group actually rooting for different racers.

I would have perceived that voice anyplace. Jenna had tracked down me.

She ran into the clinical tent, her sort, cherishing eyes meeting mine.

I could perceive she was giving a valiant effort to be solid, yet her look of dread let me know that I was not even close to affirm.

"Let them know they can't, it harms excessively," I whimpered, feeling the sharp sting of my scratches.

"You can definitely relax, Colin. Be solid for me. The specialist simply has to clear out the injuries. It will be... " Her voice followed off and her face depleted of variety.

Jenna's knees clasped. Her limp body lurched toward the ground. Fortunately, one of the attendants saw this incident and naturally supported her head, minutes before she hit the concrete. The clinical staff deserted their cleaning of my injuries, and all arrived at down to lift Jenna onto the vacant table close to me.

It was the blood. Jenna had forever been queasy around blood.

She opened her eyes befuddled. I could guess by the expression all over that she hadn't exactly sorted out why she was lying on a table with her feet in the air encompassed by clinical work force.

"Here, drink this," the specialist said delicately, giving her a cup of Gatorade.

And afterward we both burst into chuckling. In the event that there was ever a more unfortunate team, I'd never seen it. We really wanted to chortle at the craziness of the circumstance. Truth was, however, that my chuckling was more a weak effort to conceal my wrecked sentiments.

Disappointment with a capital F.

We advanced back to our lodging a couple of blocks away, Jenna conveying my scraped-up bicycle casing and me limping, enveloped by blood-drenched cloth, however attempting to track down the silver lining. Basically I hadn't broken any bones.

I went to Jenna. "I don't believe I will make the Olympics," I said, totally crude from the occasion.

"Jawline up. You got unfortunate today," she said, grinning.

"It's not simply today. Or on the other hand even the most recent four years of expert marathon, forfeiting everything for this objective. Do you understand I've been pursuing making the Olympics for more than twenty years? From that point onward I watched swimming at the 1992

Barcelona Olympics on TV as a youngster. At the point when I quit my place of employment in Chicago, everybody cautioned me this would occur. Presently I am right here, similarly as they generally anticipated. I've attempted. When am I going to own up to myself that I've fizzled?"

I stopped the tirade to pause and rest.

"You know, the swimming club used to come to Puerto Rico each colder time of year in school for our preparation trip. Being here again brings back recollections. Did I at any point educate you regarding my last university swim race?"

"I don't know. What occurred?"

I recounted her the account of that day back in 2006 at the Ivy League Championships when I'd contended in my last 100-yard breaststroke race, the perfection of fifteen years of serious swimming. Without a doubt, I'd came out on top for various Oregon State Championships as well as provincial titles, and I'd been positioned as high as fifth in the country for my age in the breaststroke. Hell, I'd been enrolled to swim at a Division I college. However, those were all steady strides toward accomplishing my genuine objective, addressing the USA in swimming at the Olympic Games.

I imparted to her how I'd fall off the last turn, prepared to leave everything in the pool that day.

Pull. Relax. Kick. Pull. Relax. Kick.

With one last stroke I flexed my fingertips and contacted the wall. I gazed up at the huge advanced scoreboard to perceive how I'd done.

"I didn't win. I broke no records. I didn't meet all requirements for the NCAA National Championships. I essentially didn't go quickly enough to meet all requirements for the Olympic preliminaries. Very much like that it was finished. Swimming, the objective, my fantasies. Done… " I followed off.

I thought back up at the scoreboard one final chance to ensure I hadn't misread the outcomes. My vision obscured. My goggles were topping off, not with chlorine-scented pool water, but rather with pungent tears…

My awareness out of nowhere snapped me back to my situation on the Antarctic ice. I was again encountering goggles brimming with pungent tears, this time frozen, and, surprisingly, through the haze, I could see Captain Rudd was a distant memory.

I went after my SAT telephone to call Jenna, not knowing what else to do.

"Is everything alright? Didn't you simply begin? Where are you?" Jenna sounded frightened through the static of the satellite association.

"I can't pull my sled. It's simply excessively weighty." I attempted to keep my voice consistent, yet I was sure Jenna could hear it break in the midst of one more surge of tears that I was unable to keep down.

I went on, "I generally realized it was conceivable I'd flop over here. I figured perhaps following thirty or forty days alone on the ice I'd be compelled to surrender for reasons unknown or other. Be that as it may, I'm still fundamentally toward the beginning line, and I as of now feel like the world's greatest disappointment. I took that large number of meetings and declared my objectives to the world, and I'm remaining here stuck on Day One. Skipper Rudd is a distant memory; I don't have any idea what to do."

Jenna stopped briefly. I heard her take a full breath, and afterward she said, "You're not a disappointment. You're out there in Antarctica. Do you have at least some idea what number of individuals never at any point venture out toward their fantasies? Recollect what we generally say… the main disappointment is in not attempting. Disregard Captain Rudd, disregard the race, disregard the media. This second is for you."

She proceeded to recommend that if I would simply come to the first waypoint a half pretty far I'd feel like I'd gained some headway. She urged me to set up my tent and get a decent night's rest.

"Tomorrow we'll refocus, and you'll make a couple of strides more. You'll go a couple of miles more," she finished up.

I did also, that. Every day for the following two months, alone on the ice. I combat, I battled, I continued to place carefully, attempting to find my direction until my apparent disappointment on Day One transformed into my most splendid accomplishment on Day Fifty-Four.

After at last passing Captain Rudd and pulling my sled 932 miles, I turned into the main individual in history to finish a completely human-controlled, unsupported performance crossing of the expanse of land of Antarctica.

HOW THIS STORY APPLIES TO YOU

Disappointment is an unavoidable truth.

Allow me to figure, you've bombed now and again. Thank heavens. It implies you took a stab at something.

On the off chance that you're like me, you presumably don't recollect figuring out how to walk, yet I can promise you this — you tumbled down a huge number of times as a little child prior to dominating the art. Envision where you'd be today on the off chance that subsequent to tumbling down interestingly your one-year-old self had quit attempting and surrendered for eternity.

From the belly we instinctively know that there's actually no such thing as disappointment — that transitory disappointments are only a progression of examples and learnings that lead to progress. In any case, time after time, as we progress in years, our cerebrums fail to remember this significant truth, and we start to fear disappointment so intensely that we quit attempting to learn and develop.

I neglected to make the Olympics.

I attempted as a swimmer and afterward again as a marathon runner. I forfeited my vocation in finance — doubtlessly arousing a lot of frustration for my loved ones — to pursue my Olympic dream. Nevertheless, I fizzled.

But I put down this book having set ten world accounts.

I always would've been unable to effectively stroll across Antarctica alone in the event that it hadn't been for the twenty years I'd spent developing my actual fortitude in accidental groundwork for that campaign. I always would've been unable to endure the fear of the Drake Passage column without honing my brain such a long time in the pool.

I've succeeded in light of the fact that I've fizzled.

I gained from my disappointments, and decided to continue pushing ahead, to continue on, to continue to point higher.

CHAPTER EIGHT

RESTRICTING BELIEF: "I DON'T KNOW WHAT TO DO."

Instinct is an exceptionally strong thing, more impressive than mind.

—STEVE JOBS

I was distant from everyone else on a cold cliff in the profundities of winter in Pakistan at 23,500 feet on K2, the world's second tallest mountain.

It was forty beneath — the sort of cool that tells you freezing to death. Tearing breezes put the windchill at less seventy, which made it intense to move, extreme to inhale, extreme to try and think. At these temps, your fingers and toes begin to feel like they have a place with another person, on the off chance that you could feel them by any means.

It was two-thirty in the evening. Several hours, without the sun, the temperature would decrease another twenty degrees.

K2 in "ordinary" summer getting over conditions is generally viewed as the world's most hazardous mountain — one out of four climbers who arrive at the culmination neglect to make it down alive — yet I was quite far from typical. I was on a mission to climb K2 in winter, an accomplishment that had never been achieved before this season. In certain years, nobody even attempted, but this year there two or three dozen climbers from a few distinct groups on the mountain expecting to snatch what the New York Times called "the last extraordinary award of high-height mountaineering."

An award like that... it addressed me. Let me know something is far off, and I'll go after it in any case, which makes sense of how I came to be separated from everyone else on that edge in the Karakoram, engaging the powerful K2, unfit to calmly inhale without feeling like I were being wounded in the lungs by an icicle.

I'd ventured out in front of my two Sherpa climbing accomplices through the Black Pyramid, a massively convoluted and uncovered segment of the Abruzzi Spur course. I'd been cutting my outfit to old, frayed ropes from seasons past — an honestly careless continue on my part, however moving at this level is shot through with risk. The key is to go ahead with just well balanced plans of action, and keeping in mind that I knew at that point I was believing my life to a shoddy old rope, I likewise knew blended in with the old ropes were a couple of segments of new rope that had been fixed by an all-Nepali group of brave, top notch climbers who'd summited only fourteen days sooner, turning into the first to climb K2 in winter and guaranteeing the award. But their prosperity hadn't decreased my aspiration to in any case arrive at the top.

Alarmingly, the rope I'd been following unexpectedly vanished underneath the hard, desolate snow. I'd been relying on those decent ropes, so I was stuck. I took a carabiner and cut my knapsack onto the finish of the rope and plunked down on it to shield me from the frozen ground while I sorted out my best course of action. Notwithstanding the savage breezes, the sky was clear. I peered down the sheer essence of the mountain into 8,000 feet of nothingness, the entire way to the valley floor. One misleading step and I'd turn into the mountain's most recent setback.

In the event that I proceeded, I'd climb blind — an unnerving idea in such amazing circumstances. Be that as it may, I wasn't without assets. I was as yet associated by radio and satellite to Base Camp, and to Jenna back home, and at the time these two marks of association felt to me like considerably more fundamental helps than the decent lines that had unexpectedly run out.

I unfastened the highest point of my knapsack and took out my radio. I turned the handle to turn it on and the screen quickly went clear in the cold air.

"Damn!"

I knew for a fact in outrageous cold that the best way to keep my gadgets working was to cover them underneath the few layers of my dress, near my body, so I'd played it safe of stashing my SAT telephone against my skin. I went after it and my heart jumped as it turned on, yet in not more than seconds the virus made that screen go dull too.

I'd never felt so alone — so completely, chillingly alone.

My legs were shudder, likely because of a mix of cold and vulnerability. I embraced my knees and stepped my feet on the ice before me to keep the blood streaming. Step, step, step... like a warrior walking set up.

My psyche dashed. The other day, my dear companion and climbing accomplice Dr. Jon Kedrowski had pivoted not long after we'd left Base Camp. The mountain had been filling his head with dull, dismal contemplations. He'd been shaken by the death of our companion Sergi Mingote, a cultivated Spanish climber who'd been at the midpoint of a years-in length push to climb the fourteen tallest tops on the planet without supplemental oxygen. Sergi had tumbled to his demise on a long time prior, only minutes after Dr. Jon and I had rappelled a similar segment — a miserable update that the mountain's rage would save nobody.

"This is risky poop, man," Dr. Jon had expressed, retaliating tears. "Something inside is telling me in the event that I continue onward, I will pass on up there."

To Dr. Jon, the perils were presently not satisfactory. As far as I might be concerned, they were essential for the arrangement. I completely regarded his choice to turn around — he could have been the main rational climber on the mountain!

"Colin," he said, "assuming you're feeling better, I actually figure you ought to continue onward."

At that time, I did as well. But at this time, cut off from the world, alone on this freezing, delicate slip of land, it seemed to me like a colder time of year attack on the angriest mountain on earth was outright franticness, and for quite a long time I considered what in blazes I was doing up here.

I sat in this manner for 90 minutes, until I saw a climber drawing nearer from underneath. I thought it may be Ming Temba Sherpa — a blessing since he was conveying a portion of our fundamental stuff. However at that point I saw that it was Juan Pablo (JP) Mohr Prieto, an unbelievable climber from Chile. JP had been Sergi's climbing accomplice, and presently not entirely settled to arrive at the highest point to respect his fallen companion.

JP was maybe the most grounded climber I knew. He moved with a persistent accuracy that was indisputable, even from a good ways. We'd turn out to be close soon after Sergi's passing, enduring a fourteen day storm while having similar eating tent at Base Camp, trading stories over vast cups of tea. He enlightened me concerning that he was so eager to invest more energy with his children in the mountains as they grew up. I appreciated the damnation out of him.

He was moving without supplemental oxygen, and he was moving gradually, intentionally. I remained to embrace him. "Extraordinary to see you, man," I said. "Beginning to ponder where everybody was. You alright?"

"My feet are so goddamn cool," he said in his highlighted English. "I'm stressed."

It dislike JP to recognize a weakness, but rather it was right there.

I said, "We want to get to Camp 3 and get you warm, however the proper rope closes here."

Camp 3, at approximately 24,000 feet, was the last camp before our highest point push — and, benevolently, JP thought he knew the way.

"I'm almost certain it's a couple hundred feet," he said, as I followed his look up the mountain. He proceeded: "We have our ice tomahawks. We can climb this stretch un-roped, yes."

He was not asking, simply say what shouldn't need to be said — clear to him, in any case. The sheer drop-offs and huge chasms to one or the other side of us would make climbing un-roped very hazardous; one misleading step would mean abrupt passing, however JP's assurance turned into my own. Before we could take off, nonetheless, we were joined on the slant by my climbing accomplices, Lakpa Temba Sherpa and Ming Temba Sherpa, as well as one more solitary climber, from Slovenia, named Tomaž Rotar.

I was accustomed to being on my own in the most remote corners of the world, however this wasn't the time or place to be going it alone, and as I set out with these different climbers I was overwhelmed with a sensation of shared strength and reason. The temperatures had decreased since I shown up on this two or three hours sooner, yet I felt somewhat less cool in the organization of these great men. We moved circumspectly without the security of the rope, evading a goliath precipice, and came to Camp 3 similarly as it was beginning to get dim, similarly as the virus drained our determination. We quickly dug two little stages to oblige my little three-man tent and JP's ultralight tent that was scarcely large enough for him, and afterward we crushed inside to get warm.

Tomaž's exploring the great outdoors gear was with his climbing accomplice, who was no place to be seen, so he took cover with me, Ming Temba, and Lakpa Temba. It was a tight fit, however we made it work.

I attempted to get the oven rolling, however the gas inside the canister was too cold to even consider lighting. I went two or three dozen matches yet couldn't get a fire. I was past baffled: the general purpose of camping out at Camp 3 for a couple of hours was to liquefy a lot of snow so we could hydrate, change into a dry sets of socks, and warm my SAT telephone and radio so I could restore contact with Dr. Jon and Jenna before the arranged culmination push that evening.

Next thing I knew, my companion Ali Sadpara jabbed his head through the tent fold and inquired as to whether he could come inside while he hung tight for his Icelandic accomplice, John Snorri Sigurjónsson, to show up with their tent. I was excited to see him — and regarded to take him in.

"He is an hour behind, I ought to think," Ali said. "I will make myself little."

There were currently five of us crushed in a three-man tent.

Ali was a mythical mountain climber, the Michael Jordan of Pakistan, a delight filled human whose grin could fill even the coldest, generally incomprehensibly swarmed tent with warmth and happiness.

As we moved to account for him, he saw me battling with the matches.

"Here," he said, chuckling, holding out his hands. "Let me."

I gave him the matches as he let me know that when he made the noteworthy first climb of Nanga Parbat in winter, he'd figured out how to warm the metal gas canister prior to endeavoring to light the oven, and for the following short time he held a lit match to the beyond canister until the fire went out, and afterward once more, and once more, until the butane streamed.

"We got this, Colin," he said, grinning. He might have implied the oven and the trip since Ali was a light soul who accepted the sky was the limit. One way or another, his grin let me know what I definitely knew: the absolute best among us are consistently ready to track down light in the haziness.

Before long, there were a lot of muted, wild eyed voices outside our tent.

"You must fuck messing with me!" I heard.

"I thought you had the tent."

"Crap, what on earth would we say we will do?"

This was going from awful to more regrettable.

All of a sudden I felt the texture of my tent shake, as a covered climber from another group unfastened my tent folds and jabbed his ice-solidified head inside. "Colin, is that you?" he wheezed. "Could we at any point come in... we have no tent, we'll freeze assuming that we stay over here any more."

Clearly, I was unable to allow these individuals to freeze, so I'd need to figure out how to assist with getting them warm, yet it was a problem and migraine in any case — a circumstance that put us all in peril. The bedlam and disarray that had been preparing outside was presently mounting inside my little sanctuary.

Each time another person requested to go along with us in our confined space, I was hit by a surge of cold air that made it hard to think, difficult to envision going back out into the evening.

At last, there were seven of us inside my three-man tent, with an eighth climber hunched in the vestibule by the front tent-folds. We were wedged in so close it was like we were maneuvering for space in a packed metro vehicle.

When finally John Snorri showed up with Ali's tent, they set up only opposite us, our front folds for all intents and purposes contacting.

Also, a similar dilemma happening in our tent currently worked out in their tent as the mercury dipped under less fifty degrees. In total, these two nylon cases were presently giving crisis safe house to more than twelve frantic ice-built up climbers.

I checked in with Dr. Jon the second I got the radio working.

"It's a flat out shitshow up here," I said. "We're crushed in so close I couldn't actually unfasten my boots to put on dry socks." The others could hear me, yet I couldn't have cared less. I expected to vent. "Who the screw moves to Camp 3 in obscurity on K2 in winter without a tent? I'm tied in with aiding each other out, yet this is a bad dream for everyone."

"That sucks, man," Dr. Jon said, with a quiet in his voice he was most likely trusting I'd coordinate.

"It more than sucks, man. I figure individuals could vanish here this evening," I shouted back wildly into the radio.

"Take a full breath. You're in a predicament, that's what I get, yet your climate window is shutting. You can in any case make the culmination, however you must escape your tent and put it all on the line."

Then, I called Jenna to check whether she could assist me with sorting things out from back home. She'd traveled to K2 Base Camp with us toward the start of the endeavor, however had since gotten back to Jackson Hole. I was glad to realize she was a ton hotter and a ton more secure than where I tracked down myself. Her voice snapped through the SAT telephone. As I stressed to hear her, I could make out the confident voices from the other few tents on that cold slant — cries of "We're going!" and "We should make it happen!"

I held the telephone out like a simpleton, figuring Jenna could hear the hints of commotion in and around my tent — not halting to understand that she could scarcely hear me.

"What's your interpretation of this present circumstance?" I asked Jenna, grasping the telephone near my head once more, requiring her objective clearness.

"I don't have a decent perused on this one, Colin," she said. "This one's all you. Go, assuming you're going. Now is the right time. Settle on the decision. Presently!"

For quite a long time, Jenna had been my eyes and ears adrift level — her "read" was my world. I relied on her to assist me with following the endless subtleties that educated each choice I looked while I was out on the edge, however this time I was all alone.

The get down on cut and I stayed there for a couple of long minutes.

From the beginning, I'd been hollering to and fro to Ali through our tents.

"What are you folks thinking?" I yelled when the call to Jenna cut out.

"We are thinking go!" Ali said. "Accompany us, Colin. We will make the top together!"

I valued Ali's energy, however I was unable to embrace it right now. I'd been tossed against the side of my tent, twisted into a fetal position, attempting to isolate myself from the scrum of individuals. The stuffed circumstances had left me incapable to rest and hydrate the manner in which I'd arranged. I was stuck at a choice point — or, all the more precisely, a hesitation point. Would it be advisable for me to forge ahead with Ali and the others and guarantee greatness in the event that we succeed? Or then again would it be advisable for me I head down to join Dr. Jon in relative wellbeing?

I shut my eyes, attempting to block out the turmoil around me. I went inside myself, resting on my long stretches of Vipassana contemplation practice, and what I found was the calm of my own breath, the quietness of my own considerations.

What is it that I need? I asked myself.

I have no clue about how long I sat nestled into that. It might have been one moment... or twenty. I was shaking to and fro, murmur reciting, "I must return home to Jenna and Jack. I must return home to Jenna and Jack." Over and over.

My better half... my canine... my family... my future.

Pretty much nothing else had any meaning.

One thing I've learned after a long period of pushing my body as far as possible: the way to knowing when to press on is to pay attention to my instinct. At the point when you know, you know. Here my instinct was advising me to avoid any unnecessary risk, however before I could follow up on it, I did a speedy self image check. All things considered, I was the person who did hard things, persevering things... unthinkable things. I needed to realize how I'd feel assuming this multitude of different climbers proceeded to the highest point and made it securely back to Base Camp. Normally, I'd pull for their protected return, however what might I let myself know if it worked out that my companions had the secret sauce on this day when I didn't?

I envisioned the scene to its most ideal end, the entire way to what I'd say on their victorious return: That was crazy. We were getting the poo beat down of us in those tents, yet you took the plunge. I'm so goddamn glad for you, every one of you.

I slithered from my tent and stuck my head into Ali's and said, "I'm not going."

He gave me a seem as though I was testing his sanity and said, "You are climbing so all things considered, Colin. You were the quickest one through the Black Pyramid today. You are solid. The highest point is our own!"

"My instinct is advising me to stop here and head down at the crack of dawn," I said. "Please accept my apologies."

I wasn't saying 'sorry' — but then I was genuinely grieved.

"Indeed, you must trust yourself," he said. Then he grinned — that splendid grin that could illuminate the night sky.

I got Ali by the shoulders and got him for a half embrace. I hoped everything would turn out great for him. Then I scrambled outside and looked as the headlamps of my companions vanished up the mountain into the evening.

Ali Sadpara... John Snorri Sigurjónsson... JP Mohr Prieto...

Those three men never returned that pivotal evening. It would be almost a half year before their frozen bodies were found. I was securely at home when that news contacted me, and I embraced Jenna and Jack really close and sobbed. Indeed, even now, as I compose this, it's beyond the realm of possibilities for me to acknowledge the size of this misfortune.

An extra misfortune occured for my companion Atanas Skatov — an observed Bulgarian climber who'd tumbled to his demise while dropping down the Black Pyramid from Camp 3 the morning after Ali, John, and JP vanished. Atanas lethally fell simply a half hour after I'd remained with him returning pictures together on our retreat to Base Camp. Counting Sergi, a sum of five individuals kicked the bucket during my experience on K2, abandoning fifteen youngsters to grow up without fathers. I didn't embark to move with these great individuals, however they'd turn out to be cherished companions throughout that six-week endeavor. Our common experience — the approaching together of our aggregate will — had generally reinforced us.

How would you get a handle on such an incredible misfortune, such a staggering misery? There is no sense in it, truly. There is simply settling — something I'm actually dealing with, obviously. What's more, as I keep on handling all that occurred, all that could have occurred, there is, in the focal point of the experience, an unmistakable, breaking update that we want to trust our instinct.

Trust it, any place it tracks down you, regardless of whether it's pointing you toward a path you hadn't at first thought of.

Jenna summarized it best in an Instagram post she made for me while I was still on K2, when she realized I was protected: "Our intuition, on the off chance that we're willing to tune in, can be the best aide in snapshots of vulnerability. Some of the time the hard call is the simple call."

HOW THIS STORY APPLIES TO YOU

At the point when you know, you know.

Doesn't make any difference on the off chance that you're on a frigid edge on K2 around mid-deciding assuming it's a good idea to continue climbing — or laying there on one more restless evening contemplating whether it's a good idea to remain in a poisonous relationship. Our life-and-passing choices aren't generally about existence and demise, as they were for me on that mountain.

But, at their center, they are.

Deciding to impart the remainder of your life to somebody who could conceivably be ideal for you will decide the extravagance of your days going ahead.

Gauging a get clear the nation over for a new position, which expects you to remove your children from their companions at a weak time in their young lives... likewise a significant choice.

Progressing forward in a business organization that doesn't appear to be working out... that could prompt monetary ruin.

The stakes can be similarly as high for you adrift level as they are at elevation, which is the reason it's so vital to pay attention to your internal voice and trust your instinct, in any event, when everybody around you is advising you to incline in another manner.

You understand what you need. You understand what you want. The enormous things throughout everyday life... the easily overlooked details throughout everyday life... you understand what will satisfy you, what will drive you forward, what will keep you down. You know when to save your butt, and when to gamble with everything. Frequently, you don't have to consider it. You simply know. Indeed you do. Yet, many individuals aren't willing to pay attention to their own instinct while settling on significant choices. All things being equal, they re-think themselves and fall into investigation loss of motion.

You've presumably been there somewhere around once in your life. You hotly work out a comprehensive rundown of advantages and disadvantages, yet the rundown turns out to be so lengthy you have no real way to get a handle on it. You request all from your companions, family, and collaborators their perspectives, yet get a reiteration of clashing perspectives. You play so on repeat in your mind that you resort to flipping a coin. Miserable however evident.

Amusingly, before you made this large number of strides, where it counts in your stomach you definitely knew the response.

Try not to let overanalyzing, others' perspectives, or chance impede your natural sureness.

One of the most risky deep, dark holes individuals fall into while they're attempting to pay attention to their stomach is confounding what they hear with their thought process is required from them. My meaning could be a little clearer. Indeed, it's not difficult to convince ourselves to accomplish something since we accept that is what others need or need from us. That could mean taking part in a speculation your brother by marriage set up on the grounds that you realize he really wants the subsidizing, despite the fact that it's a junky bargain. Or on the other hand going out drinking with a companion, despite the fact that remaining in and getting a decent night's rest would be better for your morning exercise.

At the point when I was out there on the edge at Camp 3 on K2, stuck into that little tent like a sardine, it was hard to isolate what was correct and great and valid based on what was generally anticipated of me — or, in any event, from my thought process was required from me.

The key is blocking out the commotion in your "tent" and tuning into your Possible Mindset — so you can pay attention to that quiet voice inside, letting you know what you definitely know.

Toward the day's end, you are the one in particular who understands what's on the right track for you.

I'm helped here to remember the manners in which we've come to depend on GPS innovation to get us where we're rolling. At the point when I initially began driving, GPS didn't exist. On the off chance that I came to a junction and didn't know what direction to turn, I needed to trust my internal compass.

Our choice focuses are that way, wouldn't you say? On the off chance that we can't be aware with conviction what direction to turn, we should start up our inner Google Maps application and let it guide us. Eventually, that is where every one of the factors and backup ways to go and dangerous street conditions we're confronting have proactively been put away.

You have the gear you want. You have the data you really want. The membership on your interior GPS gadget has been settled completely.

There's colossal power in realizing that you have the response — it's in your hard-wiring! Regardless of whether it pulls you from an expected result. Regardless of whether it impacts the manner in which others could see you. Regardless of whether it takes you somewhere altogether new.

Be sure about this: the major choices in your day to day existence are on you — and just on you.

Since, hello, when you realize you know.

KEY TAKEAWAY

Once in a while the hard call is the simple call

You figure you don't have any idea what to do. You have an important choice or inquiry you remain quiet about posing. Would it be a good idea for me to cut off this friendship or find employment elsewhere? Or on the other hand perhaps you believe you're prepared to have children, however you continue to let yourself know it's not the ideal opportunity. Stop unendingly posting every one of the upsides and downsides. Rip off the Band-Aid. Settle on the decision. You really do know the response. Allow your instinct to direct you.

HOW THIS APPLIES TO YOUR 12-HOUR WALK

The quietness of this walk is my gift to you. The vast majority of us are having an inner discussion with ourselves about a significant choice out of the blue. Pursue this open door, away from the bedlam and interruptions of the everyday, to reflect on it finished, ponder, and increase the volume on your inward voice. Now that you can clearly and distinctly hear it, trust what it's talking about and make a move.

WITH A POSSIBLE MINDSET,

I pay attention to my instinct. I in all actuality do know the response.

CHAPTER NINE

RESTRICTING BELIEF: "I DON'T HAVE THE RIGHT FRIENDS."

You are the normal of the five individuals you invest the most energy with.

—JIM ROHN

"We will climb Everest, man!"

The words consumed the space at the foundation of the mountain like an energizing cry. I moved in the direction of the voice and saw a person around a decade more established than me, light earthy colored hair, inviting grin, dressed for a rock solid climb. He was skipping all over, radiating with fervor.

"I'm apprehensive," the person said when we visually connected. "What about you? You great?"

I glanced around at our image postcard setting and said, "Exceptional! Stirred up to be here."

The person stood out his hand. "Marc Skalla," he said, with a Southern drone. "My companions call me Skalla. Me and my mate Paul here, we're from Atlanta." The person close to him gestured hi.

"Colin," I said, shaking Skalla's hand. "Several people I recently met, my tent-mates, they're likewise from Atlanta. Daley and Jeremy. You know them?"

"Haven't met everybody yet," Skalla said, "yet better believe it, there's a lot of cool individuals here from Atlanta, I hear."

A little, trusting that Jesse Itzler will take the mic for a few uplifting comments to start off our trip. I was clustered with a gathering of individual climbers, going to head up quite possibly of the most celebrated mountain in the locale. I glanced around at the splendid fall foliage embellishing the mountainside in orange and rust and yellow and thought, Everest never seemed to be this.

What might be compared to an Everest rising from ocean level, by lapping a similar ski mountain trail again and again.

The occasion was the brainchild of Jesse Itzler and Marc Hodulich, who were determined to tap the wellspring of human potential.

Jesse is a power of nature — a determined, bubbly soul with a capacity to get things going. Right off the bat in his vocation he'd been a rapper and a record maker, then, at that point, happened to help establish Marquis Jet and Zico coconut water, setting his standing as an effective business visionary. He likewise is a section proprietor of the Atlanta Hawks.

Marc is a power of nature himself, a previous administration expert who has effectively evolved and run various enormous scope occasions and has an elite ability for marking and promoting.

The two men had met through their children, pursuing them in and out of town to birthday celebrations and banner football training. For Marc's situation the pursuing was strict. Marc would run the four miles from his home to the field every week to mentor his children's work on, saving himself the drive in a vehicle. Jesse saw Marc's novel propensity and thought, This is somebody I ought to presumably meet.

Before long the two were discussing the intense difficulties they'd taken on. Ultramarathons. Marathons. Beginning organizations. Raising a family. Ended up, similar to a great deal of super-effective individuals, they were both consistently keeping watch for new open doors.

"You at any point considered climbing Mount Everest?" Marc shared with Jesse one evening.

"Ordinarily," Jesse said. "Yet, I have children. Don't realize that I can put myself out there like that, face that gamble."

It was a customary second, several fathers idly chattering, yet a switch had been flipped, and Marc and Jesse got to imagining that on the off chance that they couldn't make the excursion to Asia to climb Everest, perhaps they could figure out how to carry the culmination to them.

"How high is Everest?" Jesse pondered, verbally processing.

Marc researched it and said, "29 thousand and 29 feet."

"I can absolutely see it, man," Marc said. "It could be a particularly marvelous perseverance occasion, correct? Individuals could stretch their boundaries by climbing similar vertical feet as Everest, see what they have, live it up."

Jesse's large thing was to interface individuals from various foundations and set up them on shared belief. "Consider the extraordinary local area that could shape on the rear of something like this," he said. "Hard labor... that is the means by which you construct enduring companionships."

They proceeded to spitball.

"Imagine a scenario where we got a ski resort to have the occasion in summer or fall?" Marc said. "Individuals could move up and down until they hit that 29,029 number."

"I love it!" Jesse said. "Be that as it may, moving down, it'd be too unforgiving with the knees. They'd have to ride the gondola down or something to that effect."

Together, they pondered who'd pursue such an occasion, who could support it, the amount to charge for it... you know, the typical inquiries that whirl toward the beginning of another endeavor.

"One thing's without a doubt," Marc said. "Whoever emerges for something like this will be our sort of individuals."

Not long after that my telephone rang.

Jesse, Marc, and I knew one another by notoriety. A few shared companions, seeing a comparative arrangement of values and normal interests, had urged us to interface. Be that as it may, we'd never met face to face. That was going to change.

"We have this thought for an occasion we're calling 29029 Everesting," Marc expressed eagerly as he proceeded to make sense of the idea.

He proceeded, "We're offering passes to the overall population. We make them flabbergast people previously joined. Similar spirits that have the sort of enthusiasm and energy I love to be near. Our sort of individuals. You understand what I mean?"

"Better believe it. Absolutely," I said, grinning and gesturing as Marc proceeded with his pitch.

"At any rate, man, we'd very much want to welcome you as an exceptional visitor to the debut occasion in Vermont. With your experience climbing the genuine Mount Everest, you'd add a great deal to the gathering. So what is your take?"

"It's a particularly cool idea. I love it. I particularly love the accentuation on fellowship. Truly, I've been battling a piece to fabricate local area in this period of life. I'm respected by the greeting. I'll be there!"

As anticipated, Skalla was our sort of individuals. We hit it off quickly.

"Let me know something," I said, as we remained there toward the beginning line — Skalla consuming off his anxious energy, me figuring out the people who'd emerge for this test. "What brings you here?"

"Been feeling somewhat lost," Skalla shared. "Following seventeen years with a dependable everyday practice, I've been exploring a profession change as of late and I've been feeling profoundly upset. I've generally longed for climbing Mount Everest. I've perused each book about it. In any case, with two youthful girls at home, this moment isn't the perfect time for me. However, Everest in Vermont? That's what I heard and thought, man, that could truly get me back on my game."

"Have you done a great deal of perseverance type difficulties?" I asked, feeling his fervor to get everything rolling.

He giggled. "Not actually, yet I'm prepared to leave everything out there on this mountain, and figure out who I am on the opposite side of this."

All of a sudden Eminem's "Lose Yourself," one of the record-breaking extraordinary siphon up melodies, began booming from the occasion speakers. Jesse ventured to the stage at the front of the group and went into his introductory statements, advertising up the gathering.

"Here we go, individuals," he told the members. "You have 36 hours to lap Stratton Mountain multiple times. That is the stuff to climb this Everest!"

A word on the Stratton math: the path underneath the gondola we'd use for this occasion addressed an upward gain of roughly 1,700 feet. That implied we expected to climb the sloppy, all around voyaged mountain trail multiple times to "match" an Everest rising. On normal it would take around 90 to 120 minutes to finish each lap, including the ride down, which intended that assuming you moved as the night progressed, you'd have barely sufficient opportunity to accomplish the objective in the apportioned a day and a half.

Jesse finished up his promotion discourse with a line that has become one of the occasion marks: "This isn't a race. This is you against you!" He stopped one moment to let it hit home, then, at that point: "Now is the right time to discharge the tank out there. See what we as a whole are made of."

We as a whole let out a boisterous, rowdy cheer, practically like a battle cry, joined by a sprinkling of independent yells of "Charm hoo!" and "We should goooo!" and "Make something happen, 'individuals!" I was unable certainly, however it seemed to me like nobody was letting loose stronger than my new companion Skalla, who appeared as though he was tingling to be let out of the entryway.

Then Jesse drove the gathering in a commencement — "Five, four, three, two, one... go!" — and as the air horn sounded to start the trip, I applauded Skalla on the back and wished him karma.

"I'll see you out there," I said, as I climbed. "Trust you find what you're not kidding." And as I made my most memorable strides uphill, it seemed like I was on the way to finding something as well.

I found a steady speed on the principal lap. Certainly, I'd climbed Everest, yet you don't move from the base to the highest point of that Himalayan behemoth in one ceaseless push. This was a totally different sort of challenge, and I didn't exactly have the foggiest idea what's in store. I deduced, nonetheless, that for a test this long it was likely best to begin with a stew and work to a bubble, save something in the tank for hold and not consume all my matches right out of the door. One thing was clear immediately: completing 29029 planned to take some serious coarseness and constancy. There was no shortcutting that sort of vertical addition.

Regardless of the drudgery, the climate was electric.

Dance music impacted from the guide station mostly up the mountain and individual members visited between worked breaths, proceeding to ascend together.

"One lap down, sixteen to go, Colin," an energetic, grinning volunteer called out as I dumped from the gondola back at the base. She gave me some water and gave me a high five.

I didn't have any idea how she knew my name. Then I peered down and recalled that my name was imprinted on my white member chin-wiper. I chuckled to myself. In any case, the individual touch caused it to feel like we were all lifelong companions out there.

"Ensure you brand the climb board!" she shouted toward me.

Prior to scaling once more, I strolled over to a huge wooden board engraved with every one of the members' names, viewed as mine, and consumed the 29029 logo into one of the squares to record my most memorable lap. I didn't understand it at that point, yet this custom would be enormously satisfying as the weakness tightened up. Each brand checked one bit nearer to finishing the test.

The following four laps passed by abruptly of sloppy advances, grass stains, and lively fellowship. I moved with a few distinct gatherings, finding that every individual had their own remarkable story concerning why they were on the mountain.

There was a brief makeshift camp set up at the base to rest and store additional stuff. We'd all been arbitrarily relegated two tent-mates to impart crowdedness to for the end of the week.

As the sun set, I immediately dodged once more into my tent. Unfastening the fold, I was enjoyably astonished to run into Daley Ervin, one of my tent-mates. His enormous grin warmed a generally cold material asylum.

"You enjoying some time off?" he inquired.

"No, simply snatching my headlamp before it gets completely dark out there. You?"

"Same!" Daley answered. "Need to climb the following lap together?"

"Without a doubt."

We took off into the evening, our breath apparent in the virus air as we fell into an even step. I rapidly discovered that Daley was no tenderfoot when it reached perseverance challenges.

"Pause, you paddled a boat across the Atlantic Ocean?" I said. I'd knew about sea paddling, yet as of now I'd never met somebody who'd really made it happen.

"What amount of time did that require for you?" I kept, peppering him with questions.

"45 days. We broke the US matches speed record," he answered, some way or another figuring out how to impart the achievement to full modesty.

My jaw dropped. "That is amazing, man. I'd very much want to push a sea one day." another seed was planted, and another kinship was framing. We continued to trade accounts of experience as we worked uphill.

It was near 12 PM. Purposefully climbing the mountain were a variety of headlamps, similar to an enlightened insect province out for a walk. It was cold and the adrenaline flood I'd felt toward the beginning line was subsiding as the immensity of the test started to soak in. I could tell that every other person felt the same way.

Not excessively far before Daley and me were two fixed headlamps floating in the dimness, stopped lights done advancing vertical. As we drew closer, I perceived both enlightened faces. It was Skalla and his companion Paul. They were sitting. Paul gripped his right calf — not a decent sign.

"I'm squeezing quite terrible," Paul said, as we showed up on the scene. "I'm just five laps in and there's twelve to go. Not even certain I can complete this one."

Daley could perceive this person was in a great deal of torment — and as a veteran of numerous perseverance type occasions, he had a prepared determination.

"We've been perspiring a ton," Daley declared. "Likely means you're falling short on salt."

He ventured into the pocket of his running vest and took out a few salt tablets. Then, at that point, he gave them to Paul and said, "Take these. They'll cheer you up, then, at that point, we can all complete this lap together, the four of us."

"You have this! Stay with it. It's exemplary Type II tomfoolery, young men," I expressed, attempting to mobilize our new companions.

Skalla glanced back at me with a curious saying, "Type II tomfoolery? What's that?"

"Type I fun will be fun at the time. It's the sort of fun we typically contemplate, such as moving or skiing powder, perhaps sunbathing. Try not to get me wrong I love me some Type I fun, however Type II is actually my #1 sort of tomfoolery and precisely what a test like this is about. It's exhausting while it's working out, yet it turns into a day to day existence feature all things considered," I made sense of.

Daley ringed in, obviously knowing the idea as well. "In what would seem like no time, you'll drink a lager and thinking back nostalgically at how you combat through this second."

Recharged now, both Skalla and Paul stood up. Skalla brought his clench hand up high, motioned uphill, and shouted, "Type II tomfoolery... how about we go, fellas!"

We as a whole chuckled at the silliness of what we were endeavoring yet continued forward as one like we'd known one another for a really long time rather than hours. The profound connection of our common longing to finish the test pushed us vertical.

Many minutes very much like this one were working out on the mountain, all as the night progressed and into the next day. Individuals were making a special effort to help, share some water, offer consolation, show fortitude — focusing a signal of light more remarkable than any headlamp. New kinships were shaping generally around on the rear of shared battles.

I marked the rising load up for the sixteenth time. I could smell the wood consuming as smoke from the brand rose vertical toward my last square left to be checked. I hadn't dozed throughout the evening. I was overtired but excited that I had only one lap staying to highest point "Everest."

A worker took the marking iron from my tired hands. "Good job! Last lap... charm hoo. You understand what that implies, Colin?" He stopped for impact, then, at that point, shouted, "Red tucker... you acquired it!"

He took out a red chin-wiper and gave it to me. My name was imprinted on it very much like the first white one, yet the red one exhibited two additional sweet words: "Last Ascent."

My legs were worn out, my feet were shrouded in mud, my body built up with dry perspiration. Yet, in spite of that, there was all something about that red kiddie apron that provided me with the last increase in energy to ascend the mountain once again.

Members riding down in the gondola perceived the red from a higher place and yelled uplifting statements.

"You have this, sibling."

"We should go, nearly there!"

As I made my last moves to the culmination of Stratton Mountain to finish my seventeenth lap and score my first "mimicked" Everest climb to oblige my first "genuine" Everest rising, I saw Marc Hodulich remaining at the top supporting every member who came through. I'd made some paramount memories several laps with Jesse, his unique charm and humor keeping our spirits high during that time as we combat to finish the test he'd helped concoct, yet Marc hadn't been climbing. Rather he'd been going around shuffling planned operations in the background most of the end of the week to guarantee the subtleties of their vision went off easily. It was endearing to see him on the highest point taking everything in and adding to the positive energy existing apart from everything else.

He enclosed me by a giant squeeze as I arrived at the top.

"Congrats. All around good," he said, grinning. "I realize we don't have a similar degree of chance and absence of oxygen as the genuine Everest, yet what was your take of the occasion?"

"Fella, this was one helluva end of the week. Truly, such a lot of tomfoolery. It surpassed my assumptions as a whole. Individuals... amazing. What a motivating gathering. I'm so happy you all welcomed me," I said with certifiable appreciation.

"Much appreciated, Colin. Excited to hear that. It appears as though it's been a hit," he said, pulling me in briefly embrace. Then he proceeded. "This first occasion was only a proof of idea. Truly, man, we'd cherish for you to be engaged with a workable method for assisting us with developing the business in the event that you're intrigued."

"One thing is for sure, Marc," I stopped, "you and Jesse are my sort of individuals. I'd be regarded to work with you to assist with growing this occasion series. On the whole, might I at any point clean up and a rest?"

We both giggled, savoring the delight existing apart from everything else.

I didn't promptly go to my tent to drop; rather I remained on the highest point for quite a long time supporting the procession of red chin-wipers worn by this new clan of close friends as the members advanced toward the end goal.

As I remained there, one lady crossed the end goal and quickly fell into the arms of two different climbers in red pullovers — companions she'd quite recently made at the base the other day. She appeared as though she'd experienced the wringer; sweat and tears running down her face and apparently depleted, yet you could tell from the expression all over that there was no put on Earth she'd prefer be, and with no other gathering.

I strolled over and applauded her. I could hear the profound fulfillment in her voice. "I did it," she said victoriously, looking toward the sky. "I extremely can't really accept that I wrapped up. I felt quite doubtful, yet this local area pushed me along."

Daley and Skalla went too far together. We as a whole embraced and absorbed the occasion.

"Everest, child!" Skalla shouted. "Could not have possibly made it without your help."

"We did it together," Daley said with a fulfilled grin.

"Damnation no doubt, man. In any case, I need to tell the truth, I couldn't say whether I had it in me," Skalla said. "It's been an extreme year."

"Guess what? We ought to thoroughly do Leadville together," Daley said. "This mid year."

"What's Leadville?" Skalla needed to be aware.

Daley educated him regarding the Leadville 100, the acclaimed hundred-mile ultramarathon trail race in Colorado.

"Hah!" Skalla said. "You have some unacceptable person. I attempted to run a long distance race once, in my twenties. Partially through, my legs spasmed up and I strolled off the course."

"You have it in you," Daley said. "We'll prepare together. You'll see."

Remaining on that culmination, I had an inclination this was only the start of a progression of long lasting companionships. That feeling has been affirmed over the ensuing years. I count Marc, Jesse, Daley, Skalla, and a few others I met that end of the week in Vermont as a portion of my dearest companions. From that point forward we've gone on various experiences together, upheld each other through life advances, and united our families to extend the clan.

We didn't emerge from that climb thinking, Okay, we're finished. We emerged from it thinking, Okay, what's straightaway? What more would we say we are prepared to do?

The response lay at the core of these new kinships.

HOW THIS STORY APPLIES TO YOU

It's straightforward truly. You're the net result of individuals you invest your energy with.

We people aren't single animals. In any case, we flourish in the organization of others — the greater part of us. But then we should be following in some admirable people's footsteps on the off chance that we're to accomplish our best.

Indeed, it takes a town... to bring up a youngster, seek after an objective, walk a deliberate way. However, in addition to any town. Assuming you encircle yourself with individuals who reliably settle on unfortunate decisions, who are frustrated in their lives and professions and appear to be good with that mistake... indeed, then you'll presumably wind up very much like them.

On the other hand, assuming your local area is loaded up with individuals who are continuously endeavoring, pushing, coming to work on themselves or their circumstances, you'll be leaned to do likewise.

On the plane ride home to Atlanta from Vermont, Daley and Skalla earnestly committed to one another to prepare for the Leadville Trail 100 Run. They focused on it — and in focusing on it, they made a spot in their lives for one another. Not just that, they enlisted six different folks from Atlanta who'd likewise been at that initial 29029 occasion to go along with them in this new test. They called themselves the Boundless 8, and their fellowship exceeded all rational limitations subsequent to meeting that one end of the week in Vermont.

You've presumably heard a variant of this expression: "Stay nearby four moguls and you'll likely be the fifth." In a similar vein is the expression "Stay nearby four crooks and you'll most likely be the fifth."

You don't get to pick your family, however you truly do get to pick your companions. Totally, you do. Furthermore, similarly as you decide to bring them into your life, you can decide to cut the line on the off chance that a companionship is done serving you.

Do you have a close buddy from adolescence who checks every one of some unacceptable boxes for you? You meet them at the bar and make up for lost time over a beverage and you get energized and need to educate them uplifting news concerning an advancement, an interesting outing, another objective, however you're met with lack of care or perhaps demoralization. It's spirit pulverizing.

For what reason do we invest energy with individuals who don't commend our achievements and backing us in our huge dreams? What are we clutching? In the event that you can't impart your uplifting news to a close buddy and depend on getting back a steady reaction, then now is the ideal time to trade out that close buddy for another one.

Back away from kinships that appear to be barely getting by.

See, this might sound brutal, however it's on me as your manual for set out a few hard insights, and as hesitant as I am to advise you to cut off a well established friendship, that's what I know, in specific cases, doing so is pivotal to carry on with your best life.

You don't need to be horrible in the manner you end things. Be thankful for the time you had with them yet push ahead and leave the previous where it should be. The magnificence in relinquishing former connections that are hauling you down is that you're making the space for new kinships that will assist with powering your aspirations.

At the point when I glance back at the accomplishments I've achieved, I can see every one of the manners in which I've been enabled by the positive individuals in my day to day existence. They're the explanation I've remained on the world's tallest mountains and journeyed through its most barren scenes. In any event, when they're not with me, next to me, they're with me in soul. Their motivation is the underneath the-surface spike to carry on with my best life.

Find the positive individuals in your circle and leave them alone of administration to you — as you endeavor to help out to them. Search out companionships that permit you to help one another, in progress and in battle.

After that debut 29029 Everesting occasion in 2017, Marc and Jesse proposed to welcome me on as a prime supporter, to work next to them as colleagues to develop and grow 29029.

Each time we have the occasion, what never neglects to move me is the force of the local area, the bonds manufactured, and the aggregate strength of a gathering of similar individuals taking on an extraordinary test and supporting each other to overcome it.

The normal trademark that characterizes our local area isn't a-list physicality or natural actual gifts. The normal characteristics are coarseness, a longing to develop, and an enthusiasm to help others in turning into the best version of themselves.

I've been profoundly motivated by such countless 29029 members. I will always remember the one who showed up having never at any point finished a 5K. She appeared and remained on the mountain for the whole 36 hours, completing Everest not long before the end. Or on the other hand the person who shed 160 pounds while preparing to take on the test. Or on the other hand the single-leg handicapped person doing her absolute best with it in a heavy storm without offering pardons, or the lady whose spouse had as of late passed from ALS. She summited Everest in his honor.

As I would like to think 29029 draws out the best in mankind and shows what anybody can achieve with a Possible Mindset. These are the sorts of individuals I purposefully endeavor to encircle myself with.

The key is tracking down your kin — individuals who get what you're about and appear to share your qualities, interests, and objectives. Whatever you're into, there are lots of individuals who are into exactly the same thing. Search them out. On the off chance that you love to peruse, find a couple devoted perusers and begin a book club. In the event that sewing is your thing, look at the notice sheets at your nearby specialties store and pick a weaving gathering to join. On the off chance that getting over similar damn mountain a lot of times gets you moving, pursue one of our 29029 occasions.

I'm helped here to remember the "crabs in a can" hypothesis of human way of behaving. Do you know it? On the off chance that you put a few crabs in a similar pail, none will get away. The cast of crabs, on the whole, will reach resolutely with their paws to pull down any crab that is attempting to escape. They're similar to those companions in our circles who are pulling us down. At the point when we clutch these wrecked connections, we surrender to a similar can. We put a top on our deepest desires.

In the event that you've gone after this book, I'm wagering you're on a mission to end your life to an unheard of level — yet you won't ever arrive on the off chance that you encircle yourself with a lot of crabs. Many individuals need to drag others down — yet, luckily, not every person is wired like that. Track down the ideal individuals and make them your kin. However much as could be expected, form a local area of companions who push you to develop and develop.

Honestly, this isn't some hypothetical activity. It's fundamental work to open your best life.

This applies to your internet based local area too. In the event that you invest any energy via web-based entertainment, you'll know what I'm talking about. The majority of us follow individuals online who rouse us with optimistic pics and posts that impact us in a positive manner. Wellness masters, persuasive orator, VIP good examples, family and dear companions — there's a ton of strong inspire to be acquired from these people. In any case, be cautious of records that trigger you. The neighbor with the "better body"... the previous partner who is more frequently a wellspring of desire than delight... the foodie powerhouse who's continuously having the "best feast of all time."

Be straightforward with yourself about what motivates you and what presses every one of some unacceptable fastens, and answer that web-based review the manner in which you would to your genuine review. Anybody who causes you to really regret yourself, or uncertainty yourself, is not welcome in your web-based entertainment takes care of. Assuming that these individuals are setting off you, it's chance to unfollow them. At this moment. I'm certain your telephone is some place reachable as you read this, so feel free to go after it. Click unfollow — perceive how great that feels!

Regardless of what your Everest is, you're bound to accomplish it on the off chance that your local area is the aftereffect of conscious curation.

KEY TAKEAWAY

Be careful with crabs

You're the net result of individuals you invest your energy with. The cruel the truth is that as you curate your local area to account for whatever might be most ideal, it will mean concluding which connections are done serving you. Pick admirably since the choice in regards to who to keep and who to give up will outsizedly affect who you'll turn into.

HOW THIS APPLIES TO YOUR 12-HOUR WALK

At the point when you notice to your companions that you've placed the 12-Hour Walk on your schedule for your very own development, consider who pulls for you versus who lets you know this is moronic, senseless, or a waste of time. Despite the fact that you'll be going for the 12-Hour Stroll alone, realize that there's a similar worldwide local area supporting you.

WITH A POSSIBLE MINDSET,

I have the ability to pick companions who'll assist me with turning into my best self.

CHAPTER TEN

RESTRICTING BELIEF: "I DON'T HAVE ENOUGH TIME."

To accomplish incredible things, two things are required: an arrangement, and not exactly sufficient opportunity.

—LEONARD BERNSTEIN

"There's a lot of smoke around there, what's happening?" Dr. Jon yelled from the rearward sitting arrangement of our rental vehicle.

My face was inelegantly crushed against the window glass. I'd quite recently dropped in the front seat as Jenna hotly drove us south through the wide spread of mountains and desert of the Eastern Sierra. We'd left Boundary Peak that morning, directly over the Nevada line, made a beeline for Mount Whitney, the tallest top in California. I hadn't rested more than a few hours of the day throughout recent weeks, and I was currently in an unending surprise as we hustled across the USA, however Dr. Jon's words stunned me alert.

"Crap, that doesn't look great. The entire mountain appears as though it's ablaze," I shouted. "Jenna, how far would we say we are from the Mount Whitney Ranger Station?"

Jenna looked at her telephone to actually look at the GPS. She'd outlined down to the moment each step of our excursion across every one of the fifty US states.

"It appears as though we are 47 minutes out," she said.

My psyche hustled with all of the most pessimistic scenario situations. Imagine a scenario in which we can't climb. Imagine a scenario in which individuals are caught in the smoke. If this postpones us, are we going to use up all available time to break the record? So much had gone into showing up as of now. I made an honest effort to resist the urge to panic, rehashing one of my family's #1 mantras: Don't drain before you're cut! Ideally, we'd get empowering data once we showed up at the officer station to get our climbing grant.

Those 47 minutes felt like hours, however at long last we maneuvered into the parking area and ran inside. I moved toward the recreation area officer situated behind the work area. He was wearing the exemplary green jeans, dim shirt, and wide-overflowed cap.

I made an honest effort to conceal my distress and casually said, "Hi, sir, we're here to get our Whitney climbing license for now."

The administrative noise to climb Mount Whitney is shockingly confounded. It's the most noteworthy top in California as well as the most noteworthy in the lower 48 states, and accordingly the trip is sought after. The Park Service stringently restricts the stock of licenses, so we'd entered a lottery a half year sooner and been granted this grant, for July 11, 2018, as our solitary shot to climb Whitney. The date additionally turned out to be my father's 60th birthday celebration, and he'd prepared the entire year back home on his natural ranch in Hawaii to be in shape for this trip. He'd driven up independently to go along with us.

A ton was in question.

The officer turned upward. "Have you investigated?" he said with practically no trace of incongruity. "The Whitney trailhead got struck by lightning today. All that smoke is from an uncontained timberland fire. It's awful."

"How awful? Could we at any point actually climb this evening? Is there another trailhead or something?" I interfered with the officer, my uneasiness rising. I probably appeared to be really forlorn.

He gave me an irritated gaze and proceeded, "Child, I don't have the foggiest idea what else to tell you, Mother Nature is the manager over here. The mountain is shut, and there's not a chance of knowing for how long. The present moment, the need is on control."

My heart sank.

"Sir, I've move to the most elevated point in 39 states, all over the most recent fourteen days. I'm poised to break the Fifty High Points world record, yet in the event that I can't climb Whitney it'll have been in support of nothing," I shared, attempting to create some compassion or possibly give a setting to my circumstance.

"39 states in fourteen days, how's that even conceivable?" he inquired. I could see his brain attempting to do the math.

I proceeded to make sense of how Dr. Jon and I had arrived at the culmination of Denali on June 27, 2018, only fourteen days earlier. It was my second time on that amazing culmination at 20,310 feet, the snowcapped Alaskan pinnacles sparkling every which way. Whenever I'd first scaled Denali's famous slants in 2016 I was dashing to finish the last test that eventually gotten the Explorers Grand Slam and Seven Summits world records. This time I'd made the backbreaking climb to begin the clock on the "50HP" in a bid to be the quickest ever to arrive at the most elevated point in every one of the fifty US states. The clock begins when you arrive at the highest point of the main pinnacle and closures when you arrive at the highest point of the 50th. Albeit 273 individuals had finished the 50HP test already, the vast majority required years or even a very long time to do as such. I was never going to budge on estimating my time in days, not years.

We'd had the Denali culmination all to ourselves that day. It was harsh cool, yet all at once clear and brilliant. Dr. Jon had seen me, popping on his skis, and said, "Time's a ticking... we should gooooooo!" as he soared down the highest point edge.

Normally, Denali requires three to five days to plummet — most ideal situation. Yet, we didn't have that sort of extra time. I had a plane destined for Hawaii to get.

By and large, only twelve hours in the wake of remaining on the culmination, we'd skied 13,000 feet down steep and specialized territory back to the foundation of "the Great One," anticipating a bramble pilot to come remove us.

A low haze sat over the icy mass at the foundation of Denali that morning, hindering any desire for a fruitful landing. We could hear the driving force of the plane hovering above, and with each subsequent that ticked by my expectations of coming to Hawaii that day reduced. As though in a cordial wink from the Universe, the overcast cover opened momentarily, enlightening a fragment of blue sky, and, as we looked vertical, our shrubbery pilot, Chris, in a unimaginably gutsy move, shot through the hole to scoop us up from the ice sheet.

The following grouping was a haze, symbolic of the next weeks. Jenna had assembled an expert class in strategies to transform our fantasy into a reality. In any case, with such countless moving parts thus numerous miles to cover, there was no possibility the arrangement would unfurl impeccably.

We landed in Talkeetna, a little Alaskan town on the edge of Denali National Park. Ryan Kao, our 50HP videographer, was looking out for the landing area with a rental vehicle.

"Jump in! Sorry there's no chance to shower, we must leave now to make the trip to Hawaii," he said determinedly.

Despite the fact that it was simply me endeavoring to break the 50HP record, this undertaking was a certified collaboration, and everybody was completely dedicated. Dr. Jon remained behind to figure out our wet and smelling Denali gear; he wanted to get back together with me two or three weeks so we could climb the hardest tops in the West together.

Following a wild eyed two-hour drive to Anchorage and full-out run through the air terminal to our flight door, Ryan and I were the last to load onto the plane. Under 24 hours in the wake of remaining on Alaska's most elevated point, we were airborne to Hawaii.

We arrived in Kona, and labeled Hawaii's high point Mauna Kea, prior to heading straightforwardly back to the air terminal to fly back over the Pacific. Two down, 48 to go.

We advanced toward Britton Hill in Florida — a 345-foot lush hill next to a parking area, a silly differentiation to Denali — to meet the remainder of the group, figuring out how to culmination the New Mexico and Oklahoma high focuses in transit.

From that point I labeled as a large number of the East Coast tops as I could in fast progression. We had the utilization of a confidential plane for a couple of key fragments — provided by my nourishment support. In a solitary day we figured out how to pile up six state high focuses in the Southeast. However, flying was not the standard. Basically, Jenna and my dear companion Blake Brinker traveled me great many miles in a thirty-foot RV, while I attempted to make up for lost time with rest between tops, bobbing around on the pullout bed at the rear of the vehicle. There was no time for rest stops or inn breaks. I was either climbing or on the way to the following high point, in consistent movement 24 hours out of every day.

Steady movement, until Mount Whitney and this sudden end.

Subsequent to engrossing my more drawn out than arranged discourse, the officer wore an articulation that recommended he'd relaxed some.

"Like I said previously, not even one of us can make any kind of difference either way with Mother Nature's arrangement or this fire, however on the off chance that you give me your telephone number, I'll call you when the trailhead is protected and clear, and I'll respect your climbing grant on another day assuming you return here."

I realized without a doubt that this fire could last weeks, costing me the possibility establishing the 50HP standard, however the officer's statement provided me with a good omen.

Leaving the officer station, I could taste the smoke. The mercury had move to almost 100 degrees on that dry California day. We — my father, Dr. Jon, Ryan, Jenna, and I — all chose to cluster in the air-molding of my father's inn room. Like a quarterback attempting to energize the group on the last drive of the game, I attempted to project certainty, however where it counts the certainty of rout began to sneak in.

"OK, it's basically impossible that we're surrendering after all that we've experienced to arrive. I need to hear everybody's smartest thoughts."

All at once Jenna's telephone rang and a curious look cleared over her face.

"Hang tight, folks, I need to take this genuine speedy." Jenna ventured outside, yet we may as yet hear her through the paper-slender inn walls. "Truly, tomorrow?" she said, holding the telephone to her ear. "Many thanks, you have no clue about how blissful this makes me." She draped up and strolled once more into the room.

"You all are never going to think about what that's identity was," Jenna said, a wicked grin arising.

"Who?" we as a whole yelled back almost as one.

"Arizona... the storm is here right on time, Humphreys Peak is presently open! Colin, while you were begging the Whitney park officer, I recognized a tempest framework on the radar close to Flagstaff and began dealing with another arrangement."

A very dry spring had prompted authorities shutting free to Humphreys Peak, the most noteworthy point in Arizona, because of high fire risk. Early storm downpours in Arizona presently intended that with the way to California briefly shut, our karma had turned and another similarly significant entryway had quite recently opened.

Jenna was at her best in minutes like this. "Alright, I've outlined the new arrangement," she said, assuming responsibility. "We must disregard Whitney for the time being. The pilots have consented to fly us tomorrow to Arizona, however as far as we might be concerned's, the last day we can utilize the confidential plane. Colin, I actually maintain that you should move with your father on his 60th birthday celebration tomorrow; it'll simply be in Arizona all things considered. Dr. Jon, I want you to take one for the group and drive Colin's father's rental vehicle four hours back to LAX tomorrow. We'll put you on a business trip to Denver. Most of us will travel to Flagstaff first thing, and afterward I've sorted out for Blake to meet us with the RV in Cheyenne, Wyoming, where we'll get dropped off after Colin and his father highest point Arizona. From that point we ought to have the option to pass as the night progressed and hit Nebraska and Kansas by 12 PM, and meet Dr. Jon at the trailhead at Mount Elbert in Colorado at the crack of dawn."

I glanced around at everybody's face, as we each consumed what Jenna had recently spread out. I really wanted to giggle, madly, at how preposterous everything sounded. However I realized it was the best way to remain in front of the ticking clock.

With Jenna's arrangement moving, my father and I summited the most elevated top in Arizona the next morning. We remained at the top for two or three minutes, however standing up there, I maneuvered him into an embrace and shared, "Cheerful birthday, Dad. I love you. Gratitude for showing me such a huge amount about the outside throughout the long term." The previous Eagle Scout grinned back.

As the wheels of the plane landed on the landing area of a little airstrip beyond Cheyenne, I could make out Blake's outline remaining before our RV waving us in. I was excited to be brought together with Blake. Other than Jenna he'd been the nearest individual to me and my undertakings. In spite of the fact that his actual a-list virtuoso sparkles in the imaginative domain, assisting me with prearranging talks, fabricate marks, and settle complex business issues, he wasn't excessively glad to take care of business, and he'd addressed the call when I requested that he drive the RV north of 2,000 miles from the East Coast to meet us. Not at all like having an unwavering companion and comrade.

"Kid, am I happy to see you!" Blake said. "Welcome to Wyoming! Feels like it's been a lifetime since I last saw you in Portland, Maine." He laughed and enclosed me by a major embrace, his whiskery smile grinning back at me. "How about we go!" he said, motioning us into the RV.

The sun was setting as we hustled across the Great Plains, raising a ruckus around town and Kansas high focuses as the night progressed. Blake white-knuckled the controlling wheel across back roads and winding mountain passes, eyes stripped for deer out and about, and in the wake of covering 620 miles north of eleven hours, he shook me conscious at the Mount Elbert trailhead in Colorado soon after sunrise.

"Brother, get up, now is the right time to climb once more. Dr. Jon is here and all set."

I scoured my eyes, actually wearing my smelling climbing garments from the other day. I got my knapsack from the floor and staggered out the entryway of the RV.

"Welcome to my patio," Dr. Jon shouted, arms held wide over his slender six-foot-three casing. He'd experienced childhood in Vail and was a pleased Colorado local. He'd establish various standards on the state's celebrated 14,000-foot tops. "This is an additional extraordinary move for me today. It'll be my 100th 100th highest point of Mount Elbert." He wasn't joking.

At 14,439 feet, Mount Elbert is no little trip. Back in the preparation of this venture I'd realized this would be the beginning line of what we named the "Western Ultramarathon." I'd got over 42 high focuses up until this point, in fifteen days, and beside Denali, the eight excess ascensions comprised the hardest individual piles of the whole 50HP task. I was entrusted with finishing them consecutive to-back to guarantee the world record. Over the course of the following week I'd endeavor to handle 150 path miles and 50,000 vertical feet (the close to likeness climbing Everest two times from ocean level), also travel north of 4,000 miles between the pinnacles. On paper it seemed to be franticness to pull this off in the 168 hours of a solitary week. However, franticness or not, I was focused on doing my absolute best.

Dr. Jon and I took off from the Colorado trailhead on a bluebird summer day in the midst of the shocking aspen forests. Subsequent to fixing out, we high-fived and ran down the path. Going to Dr. Jon while in full step, I inquired, "What do you believe will occur with Mount Whitney? I have this premonition we will do all of this and missed the mark."

Dr. Jon has a laid-back good faith that I've figured out how to rely upon in our years as climbing accomplices. "Try not to stress over that at the present time, Colin. How about we simply stay fixed on each step. We'll find a way, I know it."

The RV was stopped at the trailhead when we returned. "Here, eat these, and we should roll." The motor was at that point running as Jenna gave us two sandwiches each and Blake gestured at us from the driver's seat, noticeably depleted from the absence of rest. Ryan was giving his all to catch these minutes on camera as we were all falling into a ridiculousness from the constant movement.

"Alright, what's straightaway? Utah, right?" I in the middle of between enormous nibbles.

"Course change!" Jenna answered, her grin developing. "Whitney is back on. The officer recently called, the fire is contained. We can utilize the grant in the event that we get you back there this evening."

In no time, we were dashing down I-70 to the Denver air terminal. Jenna declared the following stages: "I booked trips for Dr. Jon, you, and Blake to LAX. There is a rental vehicle under Blake's name. He'll drive you four hours to the mountain. Ryan and I will remain with the RV and meet you in Utah tomorrow after you've climbed Whitney."

When we showed up at the Mount Whitney trailhead, it was after 12 PM. We hammered the vehicle entryways and took off running up the path, our headlamps enlightening the way. Through the open vehicle window, Blake yelled an update: "I realize a great many people require two days to climb Whitney, however Jenna booked us a trip out of Vegas this evening. You should be all over the place in eight hours tops. I'll be here sitting tight for you when you get down. It's a four-hour drive to the air terminal after that."

Not long before dawn we arrived at the scandalous 99 curves that lead to the highest point edge. Dr. Jon recorded a video of me strolling before him. It seemed as though I was stumbling over my own feet, similar to an alcoholic staggering home from the bar.

As a matter of fact, I was nodding off while strolling — something I hadn't even known was conceivable. My eyes would automatically close, body nearly breakdown, and afterward I'd get myself in a shock not long prior to tumbling to the ground. We'd been going constant for seventeen days.

That was the situation as we advanced all over Mount Whitney so as to connect up with Blake in the parking garage, speed across Death Valley to Las Vegas, get our trip to Salt Lake City, and meet Jenna and the RV to take us to Utah's Kings Peak that evening.

Lords Peak is certainly not a specialized ascension, however it's far — almost thirty miles full circle. My young life closest companion Lucas Clarke had driven up to go along with us, and he added a genuinely necessary increase in energy. As we left the trailhead again at 12 PM, Lucas yelled, "We should go, young men... simply an easygoing long distance race as the night progressed, we got this." I stared at Dr. Jon, not expecting to address convey what we were both reasoning: This is crazy!

I want to let you know what happened that evening, however as I attempt to review it's all a tangle of trail miles, and a dawn culmination photograph to demonstrate we came to the top.

"45 down, five to go," Jenna said, welcoming our exhausted bodies again with food and energy, as we heaped once more into the RV. "Be that as it may, as you folks know, this next one is the longest. Gannett Peak in Wyoming is more than forty miles full circle, and you'll require your crampons, ice tomahawks, and rope for the culmination glacial mass." She stopped, wondering whether or not to let us know the following subtlety. "It's just a three-hour drive from here, so attempt and rest, it's a speedy circle back."

Rest didn't take a lot attempting as of now. When I plunked down, before the RV motor thundered to life, I was unconscious, the pieces of my sandwich indelicately spread over my lap.

Fourteen hours into our relentless attack on Gannett Peak (the standard agenda requires five days), Dr. Jon and I arrived at the foundation of the glacial mass and the time had come to lash on our crampons. Because of the distance of the methodology, I'd decided to wear light path shoes that weren't crampon viable. I figured I could manage, jury-fixing an answer.

Impractical notion.

A couple hundred feet up the icy mass I watched in fear as my crampon removed from my shoe and went skittering down the lofty face, halting simply creeps prior to vanishing over a gigantic precipice. Fortunately, Dr. Jon had the option to recover it. He had an extra roll of white athletic tape that we used to get the crampon back onto my shoe. My foot seemed to be a mummy from a sub-par rate thriller. We both realized this was very hazardous and tricky, however I didn't see another decision. What's more, stopping was unquestionably impossible.

"I trust that holds," I said with a slight smile, and continued to move toward the culmination.

Fortunately, hold it did, and throughout the following 36 hours we ticked off Gannett Peak in Wyoming, Borah Peak in Idaho, and Granite Peak in Montana. The last option was another ascension that normally required several days and specialized vertical-rock climbing abilities to finish. We scaled the mountain in a rebuffing fifteen hours between lightning storms.

Staggering back to the trailhead subsequent to summiting Granite, I could scarcely handle everything Jenna was saying to us. "Two additional high focuses to establish the worldwide best, Colin — yet to get you up Mount Rainier this evening, we need to get sly with the coordinated operations one final time." She proceeded, "I've booked you a business trip out of Bozeman to Seattle in a couple of hours. Blake will drive you from Sea-Tac to the trailhead. It'll be a fifteen-hour trudge for myself and Ryan in the RV, however we ought to have the option to come to Washington when you're slipping, and we'll all drive together to the last culmination in Oregon."

That evening, under seven days since we'd started the "Western Ultramarathon" in Colorado, Dr. Jon and I took off up the Muir snowfield on Mount Rainier. With its unlimited precipices and torrential slide risk, Rainier is an exemplary demonstrating ground for neighborhood mountain dwellers. I was conceived only an hour not too far off, in Olympia, Washington, and having experienced childhood in the Pacific Northwest, I'd climbed this pinnacle various times, as had Dr. Jon.

Around 3 a.m., while rock bouncing across a spring, Dr. Jon went to me and said, "I will top off my water here, you go for it. I'll make up for lost time to you before we want to rope up."

I gestured and continued to scale the snowfield, the twilight outlining the stone pinnacles and glacial masses above. Two additional hours passed. I arrived at the specialized segment where we expected to rope together for security, so I pivoted, envisioning during that time that Dr. Jon had been right behind me. Be that as it may, as I thought back there was no indication of him. No headlamp, no shadows, no impressions. Nothing.

I was separated from everyone else, and befuddled.

Dr. Jon knew this course also as anybody; he could never have gotten lost. I rested against a stone to consider my choices, and after about 60 minutes, the primary light begun to saturate the sky. I squinted and figured I could make out a figure moving vertical, yet it was 2,000 feet beneath. Could that be him? How could he wind up such a long ways behind? It will require a little while for him to contact me, I thought.

There was nothing left but to pause.

As the figure drew closer, I could guess by his step that it was unquestionably Dr. Jon. I was feeling quite a bit better yet confounded.

I yelled down to him, "What was the deal? Is it true or not that you are OK?"

His gregarious snicker reverberated up the incline. "Apologies, man, I plunked down to top off my water, and got up two hours after the fact facedown in the snow." I could see his ridiculous grin drawing nearer, and with a wink he said, "You can definitely relax, I'm very much rested now after that rest. How about we rope up and raise a ruckus around town."

Raise a ruckus around town we did, but in our depleted state moving without a doubt more slow than our typical speed.

Just a single high point stayed, in my home territory of Oregon.

Street tired however happy, Jenna met us with the RV after her lengthy drive from Montana, and as a group we drove the natural evergreen woodland streets of my young life to Mount Hood. From the day we'd fired cooking up this undertaking I'd imagined this second, getting back — in front of world record pace — to the mountain where I'd originally figured out how to ascend.

One final time Dr. Jon and I left the RV in the corner of night, to move toward Oregon's snowcapped culmination. Mostly up Dr. Jon went to me and said, "I love you, sibling, yet this is your venture, this one's all you, you have this. I'll hang tight for you down here. Go stop that world record clock!"

I enclosed him by a warm embrace, our down coats crushed against one another. "I would never have done this without all your assistance. This is the same amount of your record as it is mine."

With a sweeping of stars above, I arrived at the natural culmination slants alone a couple of hours after the fact.

"Suuuuummmmmmiiiiiittttttt!" I hollered into the fresh night sky, getting my GPS one final opportunity to check the spot and stop the clock.

More than thirteen thousand miles voyaged, every one of the fifty US state high focuses moved in another world record season of 21 days, nine hours, and 48 minutes.

Then I ventured down into my rucksack and pulled out my ultralight camping cot, crept inside, and fell into the most profound rest not too far off on the highest point.

HOW THIS STORY APPLIES TO YOU

Time is our most valuable asset.

Allow me to pose you an irregular inquiry. Have you seen every one of the 73 episodes of Game of Thrones? And each episode of Tiger King or Yellowstone?

Assuming you're similar to a great many people (myself included), your response is: Yes!

Were those shows engaging as damnation? Sure. Is it safe to say that they were vital for carrying on with your best life? Presumably not.

Again and again I hear individuals make statements as "I need more opportunity to work out" or "I need more chance to become familiar with another expertise" or "I need more opportunity to chip away at new objectives."

So let me get this straight, you've watched north of seventy hours of Game of Thrones, yet you lack opportunity and willpower to go to the exercise center or enthusiastically seek after your fantasies?

Rude awakening: you truly do have a lot of time, you're simply not focusing on your time successfully.

There are 168 hours in seven days. How long do you spend looking over web-based entertainment? How long do you spend watching thoughtless TV? How long do you spend fantasizing about carrying on with a seriously satisfying life?

I've succumbed to these time-sucks myself. I'm quite flawed.

In any case, when I glance back at my proudest accomplishments, there's one thing they all share practically speaking. In seeking after them, I slice out the superfluous to zero in my significant investment on my objectives and interests. Time is our most valuable asset. With a Possible Mindset, you'll become purposeful by they way you spend it.

I shared the narrative of 50HP with you to act as an illustration of what's conceivable in a restricted measure of time. In the event that I can arrive at the highest point of fifty tops in fifty states in three weeks, I have no question you can reprioritize your week by week timetable to account for the things that truly make a difference to you.

I'm not recommending that you ditch all that to invest all of your energy on something else entirely (except if obviously that is the sort of sensational shift you really want). Rather, I'm requesting that you make scaled down acclimations to your day to day timetable to advance the nature of your time.

Require one moment to take out your telephone and see how much screen time you've capitulated to this week. I'm staying put, feel free to look. We should do a speedy time review.

The typical individual spends around five to six hours out of every day on screens not connected with work. Five to six hours out of each day! Envision how you could manage your life assuming you removed only two of those hours from the screen every day and on second thought put them in your wellbeing, your objectives, your connections. Two hours out of each day duplicated by seven days rises to fourteen hours out of every week. That is at least sixty hours per month, and more than 700 hours of the year.

In 700 hours you could become conversant in another dialect, become the best you've at any point been, make new recollections with your family, work on that part time job you've generally imagined about, or read 100 books!

Now is the ideal opportunity to reclaim those hours and focus on the main thing to you.

In any case, the main thing?

Quite possibly of the greatest slip-up I see individuals make isn't focusing on their own taking care of oneself. We fill our days with work, gatherings, plans for the day, and childcare, neglecting to designate any opportunity to ourselves.

We're told assuming we in all actuality do save a bit of "personal time" that we're egotistical.

Our defense for making this penance is that we need to excel in our vocations, or forever show up for our children. On a superficial level there's a rationale to that. These are commendable desires. In any case, I've come to understand that consistently forfeiting taking care of oneself prompts burnout, which, amusingly, exacerbates us at the things we're forfeiting for in any case. We become more regrettable at our positions, less understanding as guardians, far off from our life partners, and by and large unfortunate and miserable.

Consider it: when we work an hour less with the goal that we can work out, we become more useful and productive at our positions. At the point when we switch off the TV and on second thought get an additional hour of rest, we awaken invigorated and are more present with our children. At the point when you're really great rendition of yourself, it's a net positive for everybody.

Focusing on taking care of oneself is, truth be told, magnanimous.

The following time you wind up saying "I need more time for myself," stop not too far off. Take a full breath and recollect that focusing on taking care of oneself is an imperative move toward carrying on with your best life.

Reality: you truly do possess sufficient energy for yourself. However, you need to hold onto it.

We should zoom out a little.

It's human instinct to shut out the certainty of death, and let ourselves know there'll be additional opportunity for either later on.

Suppose you're forty years of age. The typical future in the United States is about 78. Overall, at forty you have a larger number of years behind you than before you.

Suppose your folks live on the opposite side of the nation and they're seventy years of age. How often do you see them each year? Yet again two times perhaps — once for these special seasons, and for a long end of the week.

Assuming that is the situation, you have just sixteen additional encounters with your folks ever before they pass. I know, it's not difficult to get mooched out by that — yet that is not the point.

The fact of the matter is that time is limited. Ensure that consistently, consistently, consistently, consistently, you spend it carefully.

KEY TAKEAWAY

To come to your "high focuses," invest your energy admirably

Time isn't your adversary, it's your most valuable asset. Assess what's on your schedule, and ensure that your time is allotted to things that have maximal advantage. Your "best life" schedule isn't brimming with tasks, have tos, and shoulds, where you feel like a captive to time. Your "best life" schedule is brimming with get tos and need tos, quality occasions that fill your cup and assist you with developing, form, and revive. Remove the pointless time-sucks, and supplant them with soul-filling plan things. There are 168 hours in each week. Make the most of them.

HOW THIS APPLIES TO YOUR 12-HOUR WALK

Try not to succumb to the most well-known excuse I find out about the 12-Hour Walk: "I need more time." Unshackle yourself from that mentality. Book the sitter, utilize a get-away day from work, skirt a Sunday of watching football. Main concern: put it on your schedule and focus on it. Your best life anticipates on the opposite side of this walk. This twelve-hour interest in yourself will eventually save you gigantic measures of time from now on, as you'll streamline and focus on your time all the more really. Keep in mind, taking care of oneself is sacrificial, not self centered. You'll be a superior parent, mate, neighbor, companion, and worker having concentrated intensely on yourself and gone for the Stroll. You absolutely have to.

WITH A POSSIBLE MINDSET,

I have sufficient opportunity and I spend it admirably.

CHAPTER ELEVEN

RESTRICTING BELIEF: "I DON'T HAVE ENOUGH MONEY."

Assuming that you take a gander at what you have throughout everyday life, you'll continuously have more. In the event that you take a gander at what you don't have throughout everyday life, you won't ever have enough.

—OPRAH WINFREY

I stood adjusted on the latrine seat so that in the event that anybody came into the washroom they couldn't see my legs under the slow down entryways.

My heart hustled like I was a bank looter attempting to make a spotless escape.

Honestly, the stakes were a lot more modest, however to my 7th grade cerebrum it seemed like life and passing.

I'd recently taken a jug of Wite-Out from my instructor's work area cabinet.

I peered down toward the latrine bowl in shame at my grass-stained and scraped white Jack Purcell Converse tennis shoes. My face was still flush from the embarrassing trade prior in the corridor when my center school crush asked me, "For what reason would you say you are wearing those grimy shoes? At any rate, you want to toss those out and purchase another pair, they're modest. Jacks aren't adorable except if they're all white," she said with definitive conviction.

I was frantic to fit in, however purchasing another sets of shoes was impossible. Before the school year I'd asked my mother for another sets of Jack Purcells. I recollect my alleviation when we tracked down them at a bargain at Payless ShoeSource for $32.99. At the checkout counter my mother gave me the Converse shoe box and said, "You need to deal with these and make them last. We have no more cash for new shoes until the following year." Then she murmured faintly, "And hopefully your feet don't develop excessively fast this year."

At the particular employment of keeping those Jack Purcells spotless and unblemished I'd demonstrated horrendously deficient. So I was right here, hunched down, unscrewing the highest point of the Wite-Out bottle and purposefully painting the filthy material. As I attempted to apply the goop equitably, I supplicated that my companions would generally not notice the rough fix.

Honestly, as a youngster I generally had a good sense of safety that I'd have a rooftop over my head and food on the table, regardless of whether that food was free examples from the hipster normal food sources store that my folks both worked at. Yet, generally, cash was tight. My folks were in their mid twenties when they had my sister and me. The two of them worked all day; my father pulled all nighters and end of the week shifts, and my mother worked during the days. They substituted their timetables so one of them could be home with us kids, since childcare wasn't a choice with their restricted checks. The planned operations of making a decent living allowed for them to put resources into their marriage, and when I turned ten they separated.

Growing up, I don't recollect going on planes other than the multiple times my grandparents got us airfare to Chicago to observe Christmas with them. Nonetheless, that didn't prevent us from having a huge number of undertakings. Our undertakings incidentally turned out to be nearer to home, however I scarcely knew the distinction. My early stages were spent investigating the wild places of the Pacific Northwest.

"The outside are free," my father would agree, stacking up the old blue-and-wood-framed family minivan prior to driving us to a state park or camping area close to our home in Portland, Oregon.

What my folks needed assets they compensated for in enthusiasm and imagination. They imparted in me a conviction that assuming you need something sufficiently terrible and will really buckle down for it, nothing is far off.

At some point, when I was fourteen years of age, my stepdad, Brian — whom my mother had met while working in the normal food varieties industry — came into the family room and expressed, "Come on, kids, hop in the vehicle, there's something we need to show you." We were completely excited on the grounds that it seemed like an experience was coming our direction. Furthermore, looking back, that was more genuine than I might have at any point envisioned.

My mother and Brian explored the heavy traffic and maneuvered into a strip shopping center on the edges of Portland. My sisters and I dumped in the meager parking area. "You see that building not too far off?" Brian expressed, highlighting a fairly rumpled business property. "We've chosen to end our life reserve funds and fabricate a characteristic food varieties supermarket chain. We're betting everything on our fantasy. Our most memorable store will open here."

After years moving gradually up in the staple business, from hourly shift work to the executives, they had a dream for a superior regular food varieties idea. They were persuaded that their thought was a method for saving the planet, and they tossed around words like "neighborhood," "natural," and "reasonable" some time before a great many people understood what they were referring to.

The radiance in their eyes that day, dreaming about what they could make, left a monstrous effect on my kid mind. They looked at that old structure like it was the Taj Mahal.

My family supper table discussions during secondary school resembled taking Entrepreneurship 101. Accounting reports and deals figures were fanned out on the kitchen counter. Each night was prepared with business arranging as my mother and Brian ran thoughts by one another. We'd hear things like:

"The brand ought to be based on firm obligation to client care."

"Might we at any point manage the cost of another full-page advertising embed in the Oregonian this week?"

"We ought to take a gander at the new deals gauges before tomorrow."

Endlessly it went.

I saw the pressure engaged with choosing the number of turkeys to buy for the Thanksgiving rush, and I took in the unfavorable impacts of not selling-through a store's short-lived stock. I looked as my folks' trying thought gradually showed signs of life. The many promising and less promising times of committing completely to a fantasy were uncovered.

It was most likely no occurrence then that fifteen years after the fact, in 2015, Jenna and I strolled into a imaginative office in Portland with a $10,000 check, prepared to endanger as long as we can remember reserve funds to pursue our own fantasies.

I'd as of late requested that Jenna wed me. With the ecstatic naivete of an as of late drawn in few, we watched out from the peak where I'd gotten down on one knee, and we asked ourselves, "How would we like to spend our days? What might we at any point assemble and make together that could be satisfying and significant?"

With the acknowledgment soaking in that I planned to bomb in my endeavor to make the Olympics in marathon, I wasn't completely ready to abandon my energy for athletic pursuits. During our post-commitment conceptualize I asked Jenna, "I actually need to push my body, perhaps seek after my experience growing up fantasy about climbing Mount Everest, yet do you believe there's a method for matching that with a reason bigger than ourselves?"

It was that audacious soul that landed us at this imaginative organization. We were guided through the glass entryways of a polished gathering room. The walls were canvassed in notorious designs, worldwide Nike crusades and other high-profile projects, a sign of approval for the unmistakable clients the organization had worked with. Situated around a table were various top-level web designers and computerized creatives.

Taking a full breath, I started. "Envision moving to the culmination of the tallest mountain on every one of the seven mainlands. Envision traveling toward the North and South Poles. Not very many individuals have at any point visited these spots, considerably less have arrived at every one of them by finishing what's known as the Explorers Grand Slam." I attempted to extend certainty, since this was whenever I'd first cleared up my fantasy for a roomful of outsiders.

I proceeded, "Somewhere around fifty individuals have finished the Explorers Grand Slam, and typically they require 10 years or longer to do as such. My point is to established another worldwide best by finishing each of the endeavors consecutive in only four months, one year from now."

A couple of eyebrows rose around the room as Jenna bounced in: "Yet our bigger objective is to utilize the media openness from this task to construct a stage so we can begin a charity that rouses children to think ambitiously, put forth nervy objectives, get outside, and carry on with dynamic and sound lives." I grinned, contemplating how powerful my time in the outside as a youngster had been.

"So what's this all going to cost?" the red-haired, thin jean-clad imaginative chief asked, half-incredulous, half-fascinated. "I can't envision the coordinated operations engaged with arriving at this multitude of distant spots is modest."

"For the hard costs alone we really want to raise $500,000," I said, trying and, sadly, failing to recapture my ready tone. Making a sound as if to speak, I went on, "However we just have $10,000 to our names, so we're trusting that you can assist us with building an expert site and brand, so we can try out this plan to expected supports."

Mr. Hipster gestured and took a gander at his partners disconcertedly before he expressed a low-energy and rather clinical "I see."

Not exactly the reaction we were expecting. We immediately discovered that our $10,000 life reserve funds didn't purchase you much at an organization of this height, however we left the gathering with a handshake at any rate. Fortunately, the inventive chief showed compassion for us and consented to assist with supporting our main goal.

Back in the parking area a while later, I opened the way to our old rusted Subaru. I was re-thinking myself. "Jenna, imagine a scenario in which no one needs to support our task. We just guaranteed those folks generally our cash."

She chuckled apprehensively, winking at me, "All things considered, essentially we'll have a cool site."

Past 7/2 was the name we chose for our undertaking's image and not-for-profit. Late one evening, Jenna cunningly thought of a plan for the logo, turning the "7" into an ice hatchet. The "7" represented the Seven Summits, and the "2" for the two shafts. We'd trusted "Past" was sufficiently strong to project the effect we were taking a stab at.

Site and showcasing materials close by, we hit the roads looking for subsidizing.

I got up every morning throughout the following a half year and cold pitched organizations, web followed possible contacts on LinkedIn, and pitched each individual who'd tune in, pursuing free associations with organizations or brands that I thought should support the venture.

Nothing.

It seemed like each step prompted another impasse. The showy site was little assistance.

More often than not I was unable to try and convince anybody to take a gathering, and the times I did really persuade somebody to hear my pitch I was met with a similar reaction to my last inquiry, "So do you suppose this is the kind of thing your organization could keen on support?"

"No."

Or on the other hand a minor departure from that, "Best of luck, kid," which I came to acknowledge was only a not at all subtle and somewhat more courteous approach to saying, "No." We must've heard 100 variants of no during those long months.

Attempting to stay hopeful, we started our most memorable round of not-for-profit exceed and began visiting grade schools nearby. We shared the Grand Slam plan and welcomed educators to implant campaign content into their educational program in association with the task. In our vision, they would show examples geology, history, culture, and environment in extraordinary ways as understudies followed my campaign progressively.

As the date of my planned flight approached, I wound up remaining before a class of second graders. The room was humming as I addressed inquiries from inquisitive understudies about penguins, polar bears, and whether I could meet Santa at the North Pole. I cherished the understudies' unfiltered energy, however remaining there, realizing I was well shy of raising the assets I expected to really endeavor the Grand Slam, I started to feel like a fake.

On the off chance that I don't find sponsorship soon, I'll need to drop this entire thing, I thought, feeling crushed.

The next week, at a bistro close to our home, I ran into a companion named Angelo, who said there was someone I ought to meet. Angelo, who knew the difficulties Jenna and I were having sending off our task, went to Sunday morning turn classes, and this individual, he said, was likewise an ordinary.

"She was a hotshot sprinter before — a world record holder. Could cheer you up. At any rate, you ought to come and meet her," he said.

The next Sunday I hauled myself to the exercise center by my home. After years contending as an expert marathon runner, my self image got the better of me. Practicing in a gathering wellness class is underneath me, I contemplated. Be that as it may, I was frantic and figured I had a lot to gain by simply going for it.

As I was raising the seat on my twist bicycle, Angelo strolled over and pulled me toward the side of the room, where a lady was at that point riding hard despite the fact that the class hadn't begun. She appeared to be in her mid-fifties and was lean and incredibly fit. Sweat flickered on her arms and neck, and I had the unexpected acknowledgment that twist classes had genuine competitors in them.

"Colin, this is Kathy. Kathy, Colin."

Kathy stopped from her exercise and we shook hands.

"Kathy broke the world record for the 5K during the 1970s," Angelo said. "Kathy Mills then, at that point, university legend."

"Quite a while back," Kathy promptly said, snatching a towel and shaking her head like it wasn't so significant. "So everything that's this task Angelo has said to me about?"

I calmly inhaled. I'd recounted the story many times by then in gatherings, bistros, bars, schools, even in the road when I'd meet a few old colleagues, and however I realized I'd most likely gotten better at it, the absence of progress had begun to pester at me. Perhaps I wasn't getting things done as needs be.

Yet, as I opened my mouth that morning, everything met up and streamed out, both the energy and the clearness. I currently in a flash respected Kathy, however I wasn't pitching her, wasn't requesting a single thing from her, and that was presumably the distinction. I was only a person in a Sunday morning turn class discussing his fantasies and objectives.

And afterward for the following an hour and a half I turned. It was a fine exercise, better than I'd expected, and when it was finished, I cleared off my bicycle and strolled over to express farewell to Kathy. A person was drying off close to her.

"This is my significant other, Mark," Kathy said. He was about her age, with salt-and-pepper hair, a daintily stubbled jaw, and the vibe of a previous competitor. "Tell Mark what you're chipping away at, Colin," she said, as he and I shook hands.

So the story spilled out once more, refined down and rearranged. Around us, individuals ignored and cleaned their bicycles as they visited and got together their stuff. Furthermore, it seemed like the story — the fantasy that Jenna and I had made so cautiously — had in an odd manner expanded than we were. In the wide range of various more proper gatherings and introductions, I understood, even as I remained there talking, that I'd been attempting to compel it, get something going. Presently I just conveyed my enthusiasm without any assumptions at all.

At the point when I was finished, Mark promptly gestured. "I like this," he said. "What's more, I think it fits in all around well for certain things we've been doing at my employer."

"Extraordinary," I expressed, glad to hear any sort of welcome reaction, yet anticipating that nothing should happen to it. I'd heard an excessive number of individuals express comparable things and afterward add "best of luck, kid" toward the end.

"Here, let me get you a card," Mark expressed, twisting around and stirring through his duffel bag. "Send me an email and a connection to your site in the event that you have one and we'll talk."

I held it in my sweat-soaked hand, gazing down at it.

"Mark Parker," the card said. "CEO, Nike, Inc."

HOW THIS STORY APPLIES TO YOU

So what is your take? Did I simply luck out?

Was it nothing but karma to be perfectly positioned with flawless timing to land a Nike sponsorship — one that intensified our not-for-profit mission while permitting me to understand my fantasy about climbing Everest in transit to establishing my initial two worldwide bests for the Seven Summits and the Explorers Grand Slam in 139 days?

My response: no.

One of my mother's #1 maxims is Luck arrives at the people who are ready.

The progress of this story did not depend on karma, yet rather on steadiness and an unfaltering faith in a positive result — regardless of having the initial hundred individuals I contributed hammer the entryway my face.

In the accompanying pages I'll show you how you can utilize a Possible Mindset to understand your fantasies, how cash is plentiful and you can have it as well.

As of late, I surveyed my Instagram crowd, inquiring "What's the main thing holding up traffic of you carrying on with your best life?" Over 75% of the responses were something similar: "I need more cash." Well then, provided that this is true a large number of you have a similar seen barrier, we should discuss how you can vanquish this restricting conviction.

Prior in this book I requested that you embrace uneasiness. So it's quite reasonable that I take my own recommendation here and get out of my usual range of familiarity. These following sections are awkward for me to compose, however I share them to enlighten a significant point.

Prepare to wince.

Jenna and I have transformed that underlying $10,000 interest in ourselves into critical monetary accomplishment throughout the long term. We've fabricated various profoundly productive undertakings fixated on talking, distributing, marking bargains, as well as film and TV projects in Hollywood. Furthermore, my colleagues and I had an eight-figure exit from selling our occasions organization.

The fact of the matter is: I don't need to utilize Wite-Out on my tennis shoes any longer.

Does discussing funds, either mine or yours, cause you to feel awkward? Why would that be?

The response: we've been told, unmistakably and subliminally, our whole lives that we shouldn't discuss cash — that cash is an untouchable no subject. However by far most of us go through our waking hours wishing we had more.

Furthermore, in that lies the issue.

Society has customized us to accept purported "insights" about cash. For example, cash is the foundation of all underhanded and cash doesn't fall from the sky.

As a matter of fact, those expressions aren't bits of insight — rather, they're imbued restricting convictions.

Certainly, detestable individuals have done insidious things with cash, however cash itself isn't intrinsically malicious. From restoring infection to giving sanctuary to your family to offering the delight of a home-prepared feast, there are innumerable instances of the constructive outcomes of cash.

It is actually the case that cash doesn't in a real sense fall from the sky, yet the pith of shortage that is passed by that articulation is hurtful on to development. This moment's the best opportunity for you to change your inward discourse so you can develop monetary overflow.

Throughout everyday life, you can decide to incline toward one or the other shortage or overflow. Those with a Possible Mindset pick overflow.

We should discuss the contrast between the two.

Stephen Covey, in his top rated book The 7 Habits of Highly Effective People, makes sense of that a viewpoint that everything is limited approaches the world as far as what you can't have, while an overflow outlook sees the world as far as what you can have. It's the distinction between zeroing in on limitations versus valuable open doors.

In any case, how would you make that outlook shift toward overflow? These four stages underneath will give a guide:

1. Put forth A SPECIFIC FINANCIAL GOAL

Begin by posing yourself an unassuming inquiry like "In the event that I had all the cash I wanted and an opportunity to spend it, what might I do?"

How much cash do you really should try to understand that vision?

The key is to be explicit. Record it on paper: _____

2. Check out YOUR ASSETS

As opposed to let the world view limited by fear creep back in — posting the justifications for why you can't make your fantasy situation — begin causing a rundown of what assets you to do have.

For instance, when Jenna and I had just $10,000, we could undoubtedly have thought, There's not a chance we'll at any point have the option to raise $500,000 for our Grand Slam project. All things being equal, we got inventive, utilizing an overflow attitude to ask ourselves how we could utilize what we needed to raise more, which prompted our structure the site to draw in supports.

At the point when I say "resources," I don't just mean your bank balance. "Resources" for this situation likewise alludes to your experience, your schooling, your organization, your hard working attitude, and whatever else is at present helping you out.

Maybe you need to travel abroad for a year, however your world view limited by fear lets you know that the work market in your industry is supercompetitive and in the event that you quit the present moment, you'll always be unable to find as great of a task when you get back. An overflow mentality takes a gander at this issue in an unexpected way, seeing your decade of involvement as a resource, and trusts that when you get back from your movements you'll have the option to reemerge the work market. The existence examples you gain from your movements might try and land you a superior profession opportunity.

3. BE CLEAR ON YOUR WHY

Making statements like "I need to be rich" without a particular why seldom yields results. My why wasn't to have cash only for filling my financial balance. Rather, my enthusiasm for opportunity, encounters, and effect filled my longing to bring in cash.

What's your why? Take a stab at filling in the clear:

"I'm centered around bringing in more cash so I can...

...set up my children for school so they don't graduate with understudy obligation

...have more opportunity to seek after my leisure activities and travel

...begin a flourishing not-for-profit and reward my local area

... climb the Seven Summits... "

There's no right response, however having a particular why that you really put stock in is significant to producing overflow.

4. Make a move RELENTLESSLY

What I'm pushing isn't an easy money scam. It's conceivable, probable even, that arriving at your particular monetary objective will take time. The key: don't surrender.

When you have your particular objective at the top of the priority list, begin pursuing it consistently. Envision yourself accomplishing that result. Enlighten your loved ones. Make a little stride, regardless of how little, toward it consistently.

Your activity and day to day conviction will create energy that will assist with making your fantasies a reality. Certain individuals call this the Law of Attraction; others with a faith in powers more significant than ourselves will say, "The Universe plans to help." But there's nothing particularly charm about it. The truth of the matter is, assuming you're continuously checking the skyline, you're bound to notice an open door.

Allow me to put it another way: when you begin making a steady move with an overflow outlook and a firm confidence in a positive result, you'll give energy and oxygen to your particular objective and the particular why that connects to it — and similar individuals who can assist will with being attracted to you. In practically no time, entryways you never realized existed will open, introducing new assets and energy for your vision.

KEY TAKEAWAY

Construct your site, acknowledge overflow

Your outlook affects your ledger. Moving from a viewpoint that everything is limited to an overflow mentality will go quite far toward assisting you with arriving at your monetary objectives. At the start of your establishing long term financial stability venture, let go of your restricting convictions around cash, put forth a particular monetary objective, take stock of your resources, be sure about your why, and persistently seek after your objectives with activity.

HOW THIS APPLIES TO YOUR 12-HOUR WALK

Recall what my father said, "The outside are free." The 12-Hour Walk is intended to cost hardly anything. However long you have a couple of shoes and the will to roll out significant improvement, you have all that you require to receive the benefits of the 12-Hour Walk. The truth of the matter is, most of life's most significant encounters cost barely anything. With respect to your objectives that really do require cash, utilize the existence of the Walk to get clear on your particular goal and your why. Then, at that point, embrace an overflow mentality — it will fuel your interests.

WITH A POSSIBLE MINDSET,

I accept that cash is bountiful and I can have it as well.

CHAPTER TWELVE

RESTRICTING BELIEF: "I DON'T HAVE WHAT IT TAKES."

It isn't the mountain we overcome, yet ourselves.

—SIR EDMUND HILLARY

Occasionally surprise you like getting back finished by a vehicle while you're left at a stoplight. Walk 11, 2020, was one of those days for me.

I'd recently gotten back from my as of late suspended book visit. My PC was open kneeling down and I was looking over the day's titles, attempting to figure out all that was occurring.

Letting the cat out of the bag:

Trump Is Suspending Travel from Europe to the United States — BuzzFeed

NBA Suspends Season After Player Tests Positive for Coronavirus — NYTimes

Tom Hanks, Rita Wilson Say They've Tested Positive for the Coronavirus — FoxNews

World Health Organization Declares COVID-19 a Pandemic — TIME

"This is wild, take a gander at this," I shared with Jenna as I slid the PC across the love seat. "I don't have the foggiest idea, yet I thoroughly consider it'll all blow in a long time."

"I trust so," she answered, not trying to gaze upward from her telephone. "In any case pressing all that climbing gear for China was a monster exercise in futility." We'd went through the day pressing ice tomahawks, down suits, crampons, and 8000m climbing boots for our impending undertaking.

A couple of moments later, everything trust was run.

"Colin! I don't think we'll be going to Everest..." Jenna burst out. "Go glance at what Outside magazine recently tweeted."

Letting the cat out of the bag:

China Just Closed the North Side of Mount Everest — Outside Magazine

I covered my face with both of my hands, and interestingly started to acknowledge that the world was everlastingly different.

One year sooner, on a fresh spring day, Jenna and I had been strolling our canine, Jack, close to our home. The sun was out, however the colder time of year snow actually covered the Tetons like a white material hung over transcending models.

Casually, Jenna moved in the direction of me and said, "I know I'm not exactly a climber, but rather do you suppose it'd be feasible for me to climb Mount Everest one day?"

My eyes illuminated. We'd climbed a few pinnacles together throughout the long term. We even got connected with at 19,000 feet on a peak in Ecuador. Jenna had forever been unquestionably strong of my undertakings, however in the wake of seeing firsthand the difficulties and enduring I'd had to deal with at the closures of the Earth and on peaks, she'd never shown a lot of interest in specifically taking on these sorts of bigger endeavors.

"Are you serious?" I asked, radiating. She gestured back. "Then, hell no doubt, it's conceivable. We'd need to prepare you up the entire year, yet with the right attitude, you surely have the stuff to arrive at the highest point."

"Indeed, if I somehow managed to attempt, I'd need to move from the Chinese side, the north side. I care very little about the Nepal side. I'd never move through the Khumbu Icefall," she expressed vehemently. She was referring to a scandalous part of Everest's south side course that had killed numerous climbers.

"I get where you're coming from with the Khumbu Icefall," I said, reviewing my move through the startling ice labyrinth when I'd summited Everest from Nepal in 2016. "The Chinese side sounds perfect to me — it'll be another experience for the two of us. Assuming that you're focused on the objective, we can prepare you by the following spring."

Commit she did.

For the following year, while as yet shuffling all of the work with our organizations and assisting me with arranging the Drake Passage column, Jenna prepared for her objective of climbing Mount Everest. I showed her the essential specialized abilities while we climbed a few pinnacles together. She'd start off ahead of schedule and do laps on the mountains close to our home, and while preparing outside wasn't a choice she'd propel herself through extreme focus exercise center schedules.

She was holding nothing back, until that critical day in March 2020, when in a moment it was everywhere.

We moved to the Oregon Coast for the all out COVID lockdown that spring. Despite the fact that it was a positive time as in the 12-Hour Walk was conceived, in general it was an upsetting time for us as well as the entire world. We immediately understood that the crossing out of our campaign was insignificant.

One dark Oregon day I found Jenna drooped in the TV room. "How about we pull together," I said. "Keep your preparation and wellness up. You'll have your chance on Everest one year from now when it opens up once more."

"I've placed a ton of thought into this, Colin, and given all that is happening with COVID and the world, I genuinely don't want to prepare for Everest any longer. I'm ready to move on."

I couldn't persuade her to get back on the pony.

"I won't climb Everest. It appears as though a warning that it didn't resolve the initial occasion when me — perhaps it isn't intended to be. In any case, i'm not a climber. Furthermore, to be perfectly honest, I'd be embarrassed assuming I fallen flat and we squandered all that cash."

Adhering to her promise, she quit preparing totally.

Letting it be known:

Mount Everest to Reopen for First Climbers Post-Pandemic — CNN

"Pass me those down gloves and that cap, please," I told Jenna, pointing at a heap of stuff in our carport. It was March 11, 2021, precisely one year after COVID dropped our 2020 climbing plans, and the Everest season was formally back on.

I'd had opportunity and willpower to unload my stuff, having gotten back from K2 just the prior month. My heart was all the while hurting. During those weeks at home I'd frequently ended up gazing vacantly at nothing in particular, tears getting away from my eyes, as I attempted to get a handle on the misfortune I'd recently seen. However I was right here, stacking up my gym bags again to get back to the mountains.

"You sure you would rather not throw that clinched for good measure?" I asked, this time highlighting Jenna's down Everest culmination suit, the one she'd purchased before our arranged undertaking had been dropped the year earlier.

"I'm certain," Jenna said with certainty. "I'm eager to come on the trip to Everest Base Camp with you, Colin, however I care very little about moving after the year we've experienced."

China was as yet shut, however Nepal had as of late opened its boundaries to climbers without precedent for a year. Our strategies administrator, Arnold Coster, had liberally consented to credit the cash we'd kept to move in China the prior year if I had any desire to climb this year in Nepal. We'd felt that store was a distant memory, however it turned out we had sufficient credit to finance one climber.

Since Jenna was done climbing, that's what I concluded assuming I planned to get back to Everest I ought to have a go at something more testing than my most memorable move in 2016. Thus, I'd lay out the objective of endeavoring to turn into the main individual to ascend Mount Everest and afterward in one nonstop push climb Lhotse — the fourth tallest mountain on the planet — by navigating the common ridgelines between the two highest points, without utilizing supplemental oxygen.

Night-time spent in the carport pressing, I pulled a conveniently collapsed pile of five banners off the rack and put them on the highest point of my gym bag and zipped it shut. Each banner addressed the nation of origin of one of my five fallen companions on K2.

Jenna strolled over to me and enveloped me by her arms, saying, "Bringing those banners up to the culmination with you is a wonderful method for respecting them. I'm glad for you. I want to believe that you discover some conclusion up there."

A couple of days after we'd arrived in Nepal and cleared the neighborhood COVID quarantine conventions, we boarded a helicopter, looking as the clamoring roads of Kathmandu, loaded with mopeds and outside business sectors, vanished into the distance. We figured we wouldn't have returned to civilization for no less than two months.

We went through the following week traveling across the superb Khumbu Valley encompassed by behemoth snowcapped mountains and passing antiquated religious communities. Every day we wanted to two or three thousand feet higher, starting at 9,383 feet in the town of Lukla and consistently advancing toward Mount Everest Base Camp, situated at 17,500 feet. By then, at that point, we trusted, our bodies would be basically changed in accordance with the meager air, however there'd be a serious phase of acclimatization even after that.

It seemed like requiring a stage back in investment 100 years. There are no streets, simply a restricted and steep trail interfacing the Sherpa towns of the Khumbu Valley.

Jenna gazed in wonder, eyes wide, breathing vigorously. "I can barely oversee conveying my little rucksack at this height," she expressed similarly as a resident twisted around at his midriff drew closer, carrying on his back a few twenty-foot steel radiates that needed to weigh above and beyond 200 pounds. He traveled past us, blazing a well disposed grin. Godlike strength on full showcase.

We'd adjusted our operations so we could travel with Dr. Jon and our dear companion Mike Posner — the Grammy-selected vocalist, musician, and record maker of "I Took a Pill in Ibiza" distinction — who were climbing together. Posner brought a little guitar, and notwithstanding the actual kind of the trip, around evening time we savored the chance to sing tunes, disengage from gadgets, snicker, and recount stories over vast cups of tea.

It was a lighthearted time, yet in our sub-conscience, we knew the force and stakes that lay ahead.

On the seventh day of the journey, we peaked an edge high in the Khumbu Valley. Interestingly we could see the fluorescent diagram of the tents in Base Camp and make out the highest point edge of Everest somewhere far off, a gleaming titan overshadowing a scene of unbelievable Himalayan pinnacles.

I'd collaborated with Dawa Finjhok Sherpa, a six-time Everest summiter, to assist with supporting my no-supplemental-oxygen rising. Dawa and I had a few shared companions in the mountaineering local area and I was energized that we'd ascend together.

Dawa, with his benevolent eyes and sure disposition, remained with his blame shifting toward the monstrous glacial mass above Everest Base Camp and in his emphasized English expressed, "See around there, Jenna, that is the scandalous Khumbu Icefall. It tends to be unnerving moving there, yet I've perceived areas of strength for how are on the trip, you could climb it assuming you needed."

Jenna amiably grinned back, shaking her head. "I didn't prepare, Dawa. Headquarters is sufficiently high for me. Be that as it may, I'm certain happy I made it here. Pictures don't do this spot equity, the scale is powerful."

Over the course of the following week we subsided into life at Base Camp and started the course of acclimatization. Prior to endeavoring to move to the highest point of the world, I previously expected to scale and down the lower slants to get my body ready for the slender air in the mountain's most elevated comes to. There are four camps above Base Camp in transit to the culmination, and I'd have to invest energy at every one of them.

It was a severe cold and crisp evening. The full moon shined off the snow, illuminating our perspective on the Khumbu Icefall from Base Camp. Enveloped by our puffy down coats, beanies pulled tight over our heads, Jenna and I gazed out at a column of headlamps crisscrossing through the Icefall. One more getting over group was making a pivot up the mountain.

"You know," I said, "Dawa is correct. You could ascend the Icefall assuming you needed. You're areas of strength for bounty. Your license permits you to go as high as Camp 2." Smiling and turning upward toward the night sky, I proceeded, "What's more you think this view is great? The view from over the Icefall is beyond anything describable."

Jenna moaned. "I can't quit pondering the sixteen Sherpas who kicked the bucket in the Icefall torrential slide in 2014. I would rather not kick the bucket up there," she said. "In any case, I've been gazing at the mountain the entire week thinking about what it should be like. I would rather not live with laments." I could see her brain managing her difficulty, however I kept silent not having any desire to interfere with her continuous flow.

Following two or three minutes looking into the overhang of stars, she talked once more. "Alright, fine. I'll go up with you all sometime later, as long as you and Dawa vow to protect me."

"I guarantee," I murmured, kissing her, excited about this new turn of events.

The three of us awakened at 12 PM to move through the Khumbu Icefall — a confounding labyrinth of vertical ice and precipices — trusting the cold of night would make the problematic ice more steady.

Out of the haziness in front of us came a dismal sound. "What's that, Colin?" Jenna asked, surprised. I sparkled my headlamp toward her and could make out a stressed look all over.

"It's the ice squeaking and moving. We must move rapidly through here — it can all implode on us all of a sudden."

Then came the stepping stools.

Before us was a chasm with a sheer drop-off into an apparently endless dim opening. The main way across? A cold tightrope act over ramshackle aluminum stepping stools roped together to frame a shoddy extension.

Jenna ventured onto the first of a progression of such stepping stools that traversed the most profound and most hazardous chasms on the course. I could hear her steel crampons scratching against the rungs of the stepping stool. Each step presently had possibly critical outcomes.

"Trust your feet. You have this," I expressed, attempting to serenely guarantee her, regardless of my awful propensity for envisioning our bodies hanging there limp assuming the stepping stool ousted while we were crossing.

Her developments were justifiably speculative, venturing out over this 200 foot frosty void, yet she never let her nerves stop her. She moved with a daring persistence as the night progressed.

As the sun rose, we got around the last precipice of the Khumbu Icefall, and soon thereafter showed up to Camp 2 at 21,500 feet. Mount Everest's highest point was all the while overshadowing a mile over our heads, and Lhotse, my other goal, stood directly before us protected by a 5,000-foot close to vertical mass of ice.

The next morning Dawa and I left to burn through two evenings higher on the mountain, at Camp 3, and during that stay we contacted Camp 4 in the "Demise Zone" — a height over 26,000 feet where the human body is gradually kicking the bucket.

Jenna's license denied her from climbing any higher. Despite the fact that she'd shown only strength in getting to Camp 2, I was stressed over abandoning her for two or three days. She'd never been over 21,000 feet, and I was unable to shake the truth of how outrageous height inhabited. Up that high, it's very much normal for climbers to get height disorder, experience difficulty eating and dozing, and fly off the handle.

Fortunately, when I got back to Camp 2, I tracked down Jenna sound and upbeat.

"I've had an extraordinary several days here, simply gazing toward Everest," she said. "What a staggering spot. Perhaps one day we can return, and I can move to the culmination?" She had a glimmer in her eye that I'd never seen, as though she'd been spellbound by the wonder of her environmental factors.

"I've generally realized you have the stuff to ascend this mountain."

"At some point... " Her voice followed off as we got together our stuff to head down to Base Camp to rest.

Our bodies accustomed now, Dawa and I would trust that ideal weather conditions will make our highest point push.

What should be a couple of days' visit at Base Camp transformed into a fourteen day ultramarathon of persistence as Everest got out of the blue battered by consecutive tornadoes. During this time we got the lamentable insight about an American and a Swiss climber who both kicked the bucket during a culmination endeavor.

Jenna and I went for a stroll to clear our heads and stretch our legs, which had started to feel like Jell-O after all the sitting around idly.

A rumpled, noticeably depleted climber with a breeze dried face crossed our way. "There's an excess of snow. It's excessively breezy as high as possible; we're getting together and getting the damnation out of here," he expressed, rearranging past us.

Passing by different camps, we watched in sinking disillusionment as many groups was going with a similar decision to forsake their endeavor, in view of the unfortunate estimate and raising COVID risk in Base Camp.

"I'm not prepared to surrender. I think I'll in any case have a chance," I shared with Jenna and to myself, getting a handle on for good faith and trusting I'd get the climate window I'd require for a culmination push.

"Imagine a scenario where one day was today?" Jenna asked, an appearing illogical conclusion.

I thought back confounded, "What?"

"I think about the thing I'm attempting to say is, I realize I don't have a culmination grant. I realize the season is practically finished. I realize I didn't pack my down suit. I realize there's a high opportunity I'll come up short on the off chance that I attempt, however I can't shake this inclination. I'm as far as possible here, presently, and I couldn't say whether I'll at any point return. How about there's a way I go for the culmination?"

I halted abruptly. "I've been covertly trusting you'd say that."

I could feel a surge of fervor as I maneuvered Jenna into my arms. I proceeded, "I care about my no oxygen project, yet honestly the primary explanation I needed to return here was to impart the experience to you, similar to we'd arranged the year before. I'm sure we can make an inquiry or two and track down an additional down suit for you. Then again, I have no clue in the event that we can get a license and figure out coordinated operations this late, however I'll ask around Base Camp. I would love the idea of remaining on the highest point of the world with you. We'd have a mind blowing story to tell our grandchildren one day."

After two days we stirred to the loud solid of helicopter rotor cutting edges, trailed by a new unfamiliar voice inquiring, "Miss Jenna? Miss Jenna? Is there a Miss Jenna here?"

I unfastened our tent and popped my head outside to find a Nepali man conveying a satchel with tape outwardly that read Nepal Ministry of Tourism. Sufficiently sure, a Nepali companion at Base Camp had pulled off a marvel. The man opened the portfolio and gave Jenna a pen. "Simply sign here and you have an authority Everest grant," he said, chuckling. "Most recent grant we've at any point given, I think."

Jenna took a gander at me and snickered apprehensively. "I'm not telling my mother until we're down here securely."

Issues tackled. Time to climb.

We faced a challenge on the climate as we climbed again through the Khumbu Icefall, this time during a mounting snowstorm. Following the figure, I saw what resembled the last culmination climate window of the time moving toward in a couple of days, yet the best way to be sufficiently high on the mountain to exploit it was to gamble with an outing through the Icefall in decaying conditions.

Our goggles were lashed on and hoods pulled up close as the headwind pelted us with snow. We were strolling blind. In the enraged frigid static I could generally make out Jenna, who was only a couple of feet away. Through the whiteout, we carefully explored the maze of precipices and stepping stools, appealing to God for safe entry.

Tolerantly, following twelve hours engaging this unrelenting tempest, we recognized the orange texture of our tent in Camp 2 and moved inside, falling from fatigue.

I could scarcely hear myself thoroughly consider the ceaseless shaking of our tent posts.

"I must go to the washroom," Jenna declared.

"Be cautious," I yelled, jabbing my head out the tent entryway as Jenna left into the whirlwind.

All at once a sixty-mile-per-hour blast impacted us, and I weakly looked as Jenna was knocked off her feet and threw into a close by snowbank.

She slithered back inside, making a worthless endeavor to clean off all the snow, and afterward tunneled profound into her hiking bed, covering everything except her nose with the layers of down — barely enough to relax. "Colin, I don't know I've at any point been more awkward. The view from the top would be advised to be worth the effort," she muttered.

I smiled, pondering the 1s and 10s.

Two evenings later, as the conjecture had anticipated, the breeze at long last quieted and everything calmed, similar to a spigot when you switch off the water. We were resting head to toe, the best way to fit inside our claustrophobic tent serenely. I sat up and kissed Jenna on the brow. "Get some great rest this evening, we'll leave first thing for Camp 3, and afterward the next night for the culmination!"

Crash, bang. "Heeeeelllp!" I arose to Jenna shouting as loud as possible.

Like a waking bad dream, our tent was collapsing on top of us, and the stunning hints of a cargo train barreling past filled our ears. Bewildered, I attempted to sit up, pushing against the top of our now eviscerated tent, attempting to get a handle on the thing was occurring.

Jenna's head was stuck underneath the difficult side of the imploded tent. I felt an adrenaline flood, my cerebrum at last handling the desperate conditions.

"It's a torrential slide!" I yelled, getting Jenna's body and dislodging her head from the snowbank that had crushed into our tent.

Quietness.

As quick as it had come, it passed. A few climbers from different groups were rushing near, reviewing the harm through the sparkle of their headlamps. I found Dawa recovering a tent. "We're exceptionally fortunate I think, Colin, we just got hit by the edge of the torrential slide, no significant wounds, simply a lot of butchered tents. Attempt to nod off on the off chance that you would be able, we should discuss an arrangement in the first part of the day."

We figured out how to reerect our tent in a stopgap way for the evening, yet rest was almost unthinkable after that surge of adrenaline.

As the sun rose, Jenna sat up, her face puffy from the elevation and exhaustion. "Camp 2 sucks, how about we get the damnation out of here."

"No doubt," I concurred, surrendered to the unavoidable. "How about we have breakfast, and afterward we can move down to Base Camp and return home."

"Down?" she said with a befuddled tone, "I mean, I'm certainly not remaining here, yet I didn't come this far to just come this far. Assuming it's protected to continue climbing, we're going up!"

As we scaled to Camp 3 we were welcomed by daylight and quietness, leaving the destruction of snapped tent posts and tore texture behind.

Roosted on an unsafe frosty edge, scarcely bigger than the width of our tent, we nodded off that evening, attempting to shut out the information that assuming we got hit by a torrential slide on this little stage there'd be no enduring it.

Fortunately, the night passed unremarkably, and we proceeded with our rising that next morning to 26,000 feet.

Camp 4 is the last camp before the highest point, an unforgiving no man's land that we intended to utilize just as a transitory rest stop for a couple of hours. Our aim had been to show up at early afternoon and withdraw at twilight — moving through the whole night to arrive at the highest point the next morning ideally. Despite the fact that I'd been to Camp 4 a few times previously, there's no becoming accustomed to the weak sensation of the Death Zone. There's little any expectation of salvage in the event that anything turns out badly up there. The inclination resembles how I envision a space traveler should feel while they're drifting external the International Space Station during a spacewalk.

Regardless of the setting, Jenna gave no indication of nerves. All things considered, her uncertainty and anxiety had been supplanted by a quiet certainty.

"How are you feeling? Prepared for the culmination push?" I asked her as we clustered in our breeze battered tent at Camp 4, making last acclimations to our breathing devices and stuff. I'd joyfully surrendered my no-supplemental-oxygen Everest-Lhotse endeavor so that I'd be just about as clear and engaged as conceivable to help Jenna's trip.

Jenna seemed to be the Marshmallow Man in her acquired radiant orange down suit. She grinned back. "I realize I didn't prepare as expected for this, and I'm certain individuals will censure me, yet truly, my body areas of strength for feels. Most significant, my brain major areas of strength for feels. How about we go to the highest point," she said, snatching her knapsack and getting out of our tent into the blustery evening.

One stage. Rest. Three breaths.

Two stages. Rest. Five breaths.

Each step is hard-acquired on an Everest culmination push. We anticipated that the last push should require somewhere around twelve hours. Dawa drove the way, trailed by Jenna and afterward me. I maintained careful focus as Jenna made purposeful moves forward the precarious snow slants through the haziness. It was short thirty degrees out and a consistent breeze was blowing from our left side. We kept our hoods up to hinder the blasts and attempt to fight off frostbite.

The drawn out night passed in a wooziness of headlamp gleam and oxygen-denied considerations as we crept our direction higher on the mountain.

"Bring your hood down briefly and shift focus over to one side," I yelled, pointing off toward the east.

The principal shine of dawn was illuminating the skyline outlined by a sheer two-vertical-mile drop-off on one or the other side of us.

Jenna's crampons dove into the precarious snow as she looked out at the consumed orange skyline. With a couple of additional worked advances we peaked the South Summit, a little level roost with unhindered perspectives on the last blade edge, rough ridgeline that prompted the genuine culmination.

We sat down on this dizziness prompting stage for a couple of seconds to consistent our nerves and drink in the quality existing apart from everything else. There several dozen different climbers spread out on the course that morning, and it seemed like we had the mountain all to ourselves.

"We're close," I said, putting my arm around Jenna's shoulders. "However, this last part will be troublesome, we really want to keep on track." Not offering an excess to, the two of us knowing this last stretch to the top had killed numerous climbers.

The breeze had gotten brutally, yet there was zero chance we'd turn around now. Jenna stayed strong earnestly.

"We should complete this," she said, pulling her hood up close around her face. She focused on positive headway, her instinct advising her to block out the bewildering drop-offs and center around only the move toward front of her.

The last edge was a hindrance course of rugged stone arrangements and steep ice and snow that expected athlete like expertise and adjust to explore. Maybe adrift level the landscape would have been more straightforward to climb, however at this elevation, the easiest developments felt almost unthinkable.

Jenna pulled energetically to move over the last steep stone edge. We looked up and saw the Tibetan petitioning God signals straight ahead that noticeable our objective.

"Top of the world!" I yelled, as we made our last moves to the highest point. I held Jenna as close as possible in my arms, our grins extending as wide as the boundless skyline around us.

Jenna brought down her ice-covered veil. "I can barely handle it. I did it. We did it! I love you," she said through weighty breaths and tears.

I removed my goggles so she could see my eyes obviously. "Jenna, I've seen a few unimaginable accomplishments all through my athletic profession, yet what you just cultivated is unrivaled in my book. It's a genuine demonstration of the force of your psyche."

She kissed my frozen lips as Dawa snapped a couple of highest point photographs.

I ventured into my rucksack and raised up the nation banners of the five companions I'd lost on K2, expressing every one of their names out loud.

"I realize you've all been on this mountain previously. I miss you. I love you," I expressed, gazing up at the sky, envisioning them generally grinning down on us.

We remained on the highest point a couple of seconds longer, battered by the wild wind. Long stretches of dreaming and battling reduced to a modest bunch of minutes. Getting down securely with every one of our fingers and toes was the genuine meaning of accomplishment on Everest.

As we put on our packs and went to go down, Jenna talked over the breeze, "There were so often the recent years I never suspected I'd be here. Much obliged to you for having confidence in me constantly."

I hung over and murmured in her ear, "It's been quite an experience. I'm so glad for you. What do you say we go on a considerably more noteworthy experience?"

She glanced back at me befuddled.

"We should return home and begin a family!" I shouted out.

She wrapped me tight in her arms, blissful tears streaming again as we descended to start our next experience.

There was nothing I needed more.

HOW THIS STORY APPLIES TO YOU

Now that was a 10!

Regardless of there not being a world record or a decoration for remaining on that highest point, sharing this once-in- a-lifetime second on the highest point of the world with my better half — radiating at her with satisfaction — surpassed the fulfillment I'd encountered on the entirety of my past undertakings consolidated.

At that time, Jenna turned into the 89th American lady — and the 676th lady in history — to culmination Mount Everest.

So what does Jenna's story show about how you can arrive at the culmination of your own Mount Everest?

To start with, you don't need to be an "specialist" to accomplish extraordinary things. Second, utilize the force of steady objective setting — in the event that you can make one stride farther and point one camp higher, all of a sudden you'll show up at the top. Maybe generally significant, comprehend that the way to progress is probably not going to be direct, and that getting where you need to go will quite often involve conquering numerous restricting convictions.

Every one of the past sections zeroed in on a solitary restricting conviction with the goal that you have the devices to beat any given one when it emerges. Yet, Jenna's experience shows us the truth: restricting convictions seldom travel solo. Rather, they will quite often bunch together, so you should be prepared to all the while recognize and defeat a large number.

On the off chance that you're basically my age, you most likely recall playing that old arcade game Whac-A-Mole. Each time one of the moles sprung up, you took your dark hammer and wrecked it. Definitely, all of a sudden, another mole would spring back.

It is very much like that to Battle our restricting convictions. Distinguishing and defeating genuine Whac-A-Moles is, basically, about mental strength — about fostering a Possible Mindset.

Yet, how would we do that?

The main muscle any of us has is the six creeps between our ears.

I utilize the word muscle purposefully here. Naturally we know that to reinforce our biceps, we want to go to the exercise center and lift loads. Sadly, despite the fact that a similar guideline holds for our brains, we seldom follow up on it. Rather, we loosen up in the zone of agreeable smugness and let our psychological muscle decay.

To expand the strength of your brain, it's fundamental that you take it to the exercise center, do your reps on the psychological seat press. Opening your best life relies upon it.

Which takes us back to the 12-Hour Walk. On its surface the Walk might appear to be an activity for your calves, quads, and glute muscles. Be that as it may, it's not. The 12-Hour Walk is intended to practice the main muscle you have: your brain.

By focusing on this test, you'll kick off your psyche — shock it into deliberate action. I like to consider this experience a mobile reflection — one that will crystalize each of the examples in this book. By putting one day in your psychological preparation, you'll have the option to springboard into your future furnished with a Possible Mindset to conquer life's biggest snags.

In the event that somebody asks you for what good reason you're requiring on this 12-Hour Walk, your response is basic: "I'm preparing my psyche."

Similarly as I was excited to show Jenna the view from Everest's highest point — to see her completely display a Possible Mindset — I'm eager to consider the individual you'll be the point at which you get back from the 12-Hour Walk. Plan to meet a new, more certain you.

Now is the ideal opportunity to leave the safe place of your sofa and trade your shoes for shoes. Prepare to figure out how to embrace the 1s and relish the 10s that a great many people won't ever get to encounter.

Your Possible Mindset will advise you that no doubt about it or anything it is you need to be. You're not a fraud, so guarantee your character. Know that there's both adequate time and furthermore an overflow of cash to assist you with accomplishing anything you want.

As you step into the field, there'll be some hard labor — and perhaps in the event that it's the coldest part of the year while you're going for your Stroll, a few frozen tears. Yet, you'll before long grasp that "not the pundit counts," particularly when you're upheld by a steady local area. Simply try to avoid crabs.

You currently know that disappointment can't actually exist. The main disappointment is in not attempting. As your feeling of dread toward disappointment dissolves away, you'll continue to endure regardless, until the situation fits properly: Failure + Perseverance = Success.

At the point when you opened The 12-Hour Walk, you probably felt some misgiving. You contemplated whether this challenge was truly inside your scope. Since you're actually perusing, it shows that your response is yes. Any reasonable person would agree it's as of now not a hard call — there are no more upsides and downsides to gauge.

Your instinct is your directing power. Trust it.

KEY TAKEAWAY

Make "at some point" today

It's not difficult to put off carrying on with your best life presently, permitting restricting convictions to hinder making a quick move. We can continuously track down motivations to contract the present for the future — to beguile ourselves with the story that one day we'll resign and travel, one day we'll carve out the opportunity to seek after our fantasies, one day we'll climb our Mount Everest. However, as Jenna understood, remaining at the foundation of that Himalayan behemoth, there's nothing preventing you from making "at some point" today.

HOW THIS APPLIES TO YOUR 12-HOUR WALK

The 12-Hour Walk is a substitute for your Everest. At the point when you focus on it, you'll have to confront and beaten the restricting convictions that have been keeping you down. By finishing the Walk, you'll have manufactured a Possible Mindset and be prepared to climb any Everest you want.

WITH A POSSIBLE MINDSET,

I have the stuff to climb my Everest.

PART III
COMMIT

Epilog

All genuinely extraordinary contemplations are imagined while strolling.

—FRIEDRICH NIETZSCHE

You didn't think I planned to leave you hanging, did you?

I began this book with an inquiry:

"What's your Everest?"

As your aide, it appears to be quite reasonable that I answer that second guess myself.

I completely hope to ascend a lot more mountains and keep on taking on undertakings in remote corners of the world. Those undertakings light me up, show me, give inspiration and profound satisfaction, and consistently remind me what makes the biggest difference.

But then my next Everest may not be what you'd have speculated. Unintentionally, however, it's something you can have a significant impact in.

So here goes: my Everest is to motivate ten million individuals to finish the 12-Hour Walk.

A reality where that happens — presently, that is one I seek to reside in. It's a world brimming with individuals carrying on with their best lives — loaded up with reason, local area, sympathy, love, and boldness. It's an existence where "the mass of men" (all humanity) sing their melodies while transcending "lives of calm urgency."

So what do you say? Is it safe to say that you are prepared to defeat the restricting convictions that are keeping you down and open your Possible Mindset?

The ideal opportunity for sharing my accounts has reached a conclusion. Presently it's the ideal opportunity for you to creator the following part of your novel story.

You can definitely relax, you're in good company. I'll in any case be here to direct you, and there's a worldwide local area of 12-Hour Walkers prepared to help you. Embrace the experience ahead.

Simply don't overthink it. Examine the last QR code or visit the connection 12hourwalk.com/commit and put the Walk on your schedule today. The more you stand by, the more outlandish you are to utilize the energy of this second to start enduring positive change.

Retaliate against those restricting convictions that are springing up.

Contribute one day. Your best life is standing by.

Venture out RIGHT NOW AND COMMIT TO

Affirmations

Jenna B, my first love. Much obliged to you for your ceaseless help. I'm profoundly appreciative to stroll adjacent to you as your accomplice throughout everyday life and business. You move me day to day with your solidarity, astuteness, and innovativeness. The 12-Hour Walk wouldn't be what it is without constantly and commitment you've spent on this thought. Much thanks to you for remaining up such countless late evenings, understanding drafts, altering sections, and further developing the book page by page, also your immovable vision for the cover plan. Limitless love, my dear — here's to proceeding to add sections to our romantic tale.

Blake Brinker, my ride or bite the dust. You're a genuine inventive expert. Any individual expecting to carry a major thought into the world would be fortunate to have you in their corner. It's been a genuine distinction to work with you to sustain this thought — the 12-Hour Walk — from initiation to completion. In addition to the fact that you are one of my closest companions, yet additionally perhaps of my most prominent educator. I'm endlessly appreciative for our numerous joint efforts throughout the long term, and I anticipate a lot more days playing in the "control stall" together. Gratitude for being the underlying willing guinea pig for the Walk. I trust millions will eventually finish it, yet you will constantly be the first!

An exceptional thanks to Sarah Passick and Celeste Fine, my unique scholarly specialists. I'm thankful for your confidence in my thoughts and for assisting me with changing them into books. It's an extraordinary joy to work with you. Much thanks to you to the whole group at Park and Fine Literary and Media.

Much thanks to you to the entire distributing group at Scribner and Simon and Schuster. Specifically, my supervisor, Rick Horgan, and distributer, Nan Graham. Much thanks to you to Jon Karp for advocating my work from the very beginning. It has been a delight to carry various books into the world with all of you.

Extra on account of Ali Rogers for your video-altering virtuoso and your assistance in fostering the QR code content. To the Luum Studio group and my dear companion Paul Tannenbaum for building the advanced biological system for the 12-Hour Walk. To Dan Paiser for your initial commitments to the original copy. What's more, to my inward circle gathering of advance perusers and test walkers for assisting me with working on this idea:

Donna Besaw, Danielle Bloch, Eileen Brady, David Brinker, Henry Cadwalader, Matt Chandler, Drew Christopher, Lucas Clarke, Kelly Cooper, Eric Eriksen, Lindsey Fielding, Lynn Greico, Marc Hodulich, Daniel Jeydel, Nate Keating, Sadie Morrison, Alejandro Navia, Tim O'Connor, Ali Rogers, Brian Rohter, Laurie Skalla, Marc Skalla, Andrew Spaulding, Danielle Spaulding, David Spaulding, and Caleb Spaulding.

Last, I need to thank you, the peruser. This book was composed for you. Much obliged to you for your trust and your boldness in requiring on the 12-Hour Walk. I can hardly stand by to see what you achieve with your Possible Mindset.

Made in the USA
Monee, IL
06 September 2022